The
Jill Dando
Murder Mystery

Thomas McKenzie

Contents

INTRODUCTION

The murder of the television presenter Jill Dando shocked Britain in 1999. But who really killed her? Was it a professional hitman or a disturbed stalker? Was it a Serb hit squad? Was it an establishment conspiracy? There are certainly no shortage of theories. In this book we shall attempt to solve this mystery once and for all.

CHAPTER ONE

In the late 1990s, the broadcaster Jill Dando was one of the most recognisable and famous faces in Britain thanks mainly to her duties as a newsreader for the BBC. Dando was born on November 9, 1961, in Weston-super-Mare, Somerset, England. She began her career at the BBC as a radio researcher before moving on to television presenting. Dando's breakthrough came in 1988 when she joined the popular morning TV show "BBC Breakfast News." Her professionalism and warm personality made her a hit with audiences, and she quickly became a household name. A lot more people watched 'traditional' television back then than they do today (in our modern streaming and YouTube obsessed age) and so Jill Dando was very famous indeed. If you lived in Britain in 1999 and owned a television then you would certainly have known who Jill Dando was.

It wasn't just reading the news that had made Jill Dando so famous. Dando also hosted Crimewatch (a show which highlighted unsolved crimes and appeals for fresh information to catch criminals) and the travel show Holiday. Dando had also been on Masterchef, The Royal Variety Performance, Blankety Blank, Countdown, The Antiques Roadshow, children's television, (as we noted) breakfast television, Noel's House Party, and Points of View. As if that wasn't enough she had also been part of the BBC's election night coverage in both 1992 and 1997. There was seemingly no escape from Jill Dando. She was literally all over the place. Dando was one of the most high profile television presenters in the country and everyone knew who she was. Dando was the BBC's Golden Girl and the face of the corporation. She was broadcasting royalty.

Jill Dando was destined to be one of those people who is on

television forever. She was never going to be short of work. Status as a national treasure and royal gongs surely awaited. She was professional, attractive, experienced, and good at her job. Dando was one of those presenters who elicited trust from her audience. She seemed friendly and likeable and projected warmth. Well, fate has a funny way sometimes of ruining all the plans that someone might have. Jill Dando might have been one of the most famous people in the country in 1999 but unknown to her she didn't have much longer to live. Her death was swift and perplexing. It was so perplexing that nearly 25 years later no one has actually worked out who killed her.

On the morning of the 26th of April 1999, Jill Dando was shot dead outside of her old home in Fulham, London. She was 37 years-old. To say this was an unexpected and strange news story would be an understatement indeed. Celebrities, sadly, do get murdered from time to time (usually by nutty fans *) but Jill Dando was just about the last person you'd expect to join the list. Dando was a fairly 'neutral' sort of celebrity. She wasn't controversial or opinionated. She wasn't even a sex symbol really. She was the girl next door. The friendly neighbour. Dando led a perfectly ordinary life away from television. She did her own shopping and didn't act like a celebrity at all. The tabloids never had anything juicy about her private life to report. Jill Dando was literally the last person you'd expect to be killed by a deranged fan. You could understand why female pop stars or actors might attract nutty stalkers but Jill Dando? Right from the very start there was something about the 'nutty fan' theory in relation to her murder which didn't quite ring true.

Fulham, where Dando was murdered, is a suburban area located in the London Borough of Hammersmith and Fulham, in southwest London. It is situated by the River

Thames and is known for its affluent residential streets, beautiful parks, and close proximity to central London. Fulham has a rich history, with settlements dating back to the Neolithic era. It was an important trading port during the Middle Ages and has been a sought-after residential area since the 18th century. The area is known for its Victorian and Edwardian terraced houses, as well as more modern apartments. In terms of amenities, Fulham offers a range of shops, restaurants, cafes, and pubs, particularly along Fulham Road and New Kings Road. It is also home to Craven Cottage, the stadium of Fulham Football Club.

The regular daytime television schedule on the BBC was interrupted with a surreal newsflash about Jill Dando's murder which informed viewers of this rather startling and bizarre piece of news. Anyone watching at the time must have had the same thought which was soon to occupy the police. Why on earth would anyone want to kill Jill Dando? That was to prove a question which rather perplexed the police - not to mention more than one court. It was a shocking and baffling murder. Theories relating to the murder were soon abounding. As we shall discuss later, some of these were outlandish and speculative and some were plausible. Others were ludicrous conspiracy theories which had the establishment (who were shapeshifting reptiles no doubt) putting a contract on Jill Dando's head because she had uncovered some huge conspiracy. These theories were truly a waste of everyone's time and inspired some crackpot YouTube videos.

A lot of people immediately zeroed in on Jill Dando's role as a presenter on Crimewatch as a possible motive. Crimewatch is a television show that aired on BBC One from 1984 until 2017. The show focused on helping the police solve and prevent crime by appealing to the public for information and assistance. It featured reconstructions of unsolved crimes, appeals for information, and crime prevention advice. Crimewatch often involved interviews with detectives and victims' families, aiming to generate leads and gather new evidence. The show became known for its distinctive theme music and the iconic slogan, "Don't have nightmares, do sleep well." Over the years, Crimewatch helped solve numerous high-profile cases and played a significant role in raising public awareness about crime and the importance of community help in solving them.

Jill Dando had hosted a BBC show which was designed to catch criminals. Perhaps someone in the criminal fraternity had developed a grudge against Dando in relation to specific investigations activated by Crimewatch? One obvious potential problem with this theory though is that Nick Ross had been hosting Crimewatch for a lot longer than Jill Dando. If some embittered criminal was angered by Crimewatch why not kill Nick Ross? Nick Ross actually said this himself. He didn't believe Crimewatch was a factor in Dando's death. Well, later in the book we shall look at the Crimewatch angle and examine the arguments for and against this theory.

The murder of Jill Dando could not have come at a worse time for Scotland Yard. That same month had seen a series of nail bombings targeted at London's minority communities. Scotland Yard had allocated extensive resources into finding the lunatic responsible for these attacks but now they were suddenly under intense pressure too to find Jill Dando's killer. The London nail bombings of 1999 were a series of three bombing attacks. The attacks were carried out by a far-right extremist named David Copeland. The first attack occurred on April 17, 1999, in Brixton, a predominantly Afro-Caribbean community.

Copeland placed a homemade nail bomb in a bag and left it outside the Iceland supermarket located on Electric Avenue. The bomb exploded, injuring 48 people, causing one death and significant damage to nearby buildings.

The second attack took place on April 24, 1999, in Brick Lane, which has a large South Asian population. Copeland again used a homemade nail bomb, placing it in an unattended sports bag and leaving it on the street. The bomb detonated near the entrance of the Admiral Duncan pub, injuring 13 people and killing three individuals, including a pregnant woman. The third and final attack occurred on April 30, 1999, in the Admiral Duncan pub in Soho, an area known for its LGBTQ+ community. Copeland detonated a homemade nail bomb inside the pub, causing significant damage and killing three people, including a pregnant woman.

These attacks sparked fear and panic within the targeted communities and raised concerns about far-right extremism in the United Kingdom. Copeland's bombing campaign was motivated by his hatred towards minority communities, as he believed that immigrants and minorities threatened the white British population. David Copeland was arrested on May 30, 1999, following a manhunt by the police. In 2000, he was convicted of murder and causing explosions with intent to endanger life. He was sentenced to six concurrent life sentences in prison, with a recommendation that he should never be released. Despite the terror and mayhem created by the disturbed and delusional David Copeland, considerable resources were also allocated to the murder investigation into Jill Dando's murder. It was the biggest investigation by a British police force since The Yorkshire Ripper case a few decades back.

The killer had shot Jill Dando in side of the head (as she put the key in her door to go inside - Dando actually had three locks on her door, presumably for security reasons) and then quickly fled the scene. Helen Doble, a neighbour, found Jill Dando's body about fourteen minutes later. Jill Dando was taken to Charing Cross Hospital and pronounced dead just after one in the afternoon. The murder scene, in terms of forensic evidence, had been unavoidably contaminated by the paramedics who tried to save Jill Dando. There was nothing that could be done about this. They obviously had to try and save Dando. This wasn't the time to think about forensic evidence.

A single ejected 9mm cartridge case was found at the scene. This has created endless debate over whether or not the murder was committed by a professional killer or an opportunistic amateur who was stalking Dando. Some believe a professional would not have left a cartridge at the scene but one can counter this argument by pointing out that the gun was never traced. The bullet came out at the right side of Dando's head. There was a lot of blood on the front garden (not that there was much of a garden) path when she was found. The gun, despite an extensive police search for the murder weapon, was never found. The presumption is that the killer threw it in the river. A rather interesting if far-fetched theory is that the killer might have posted the gun out of the country after the murder. This though would suggest a foreign connection and would a gun in a parcel really have got through the mail delivery system?

One slightly puzzling detail right away was that Dando was rarely at this Fulham house and preparing to sell it. How did the murderer know she would be there that specific day? Jill Dando now lived with her doctor fiancée Alan Farthing in his property at Bedford Close, Chiswick - about three miles away. Dr Alan Farthing is a prominent gynaecologist and obstetrician. He is best known for his work as the gynaecologist to the British royal family. Dr Farthing served as the surgeon-gynaecologist to Queen Elizabeth II from 2008 to 2013 and continued to work for the royal family until 2018. He is also a consultant gynaecologist at King Edward VII's Hospital in London and Chelsea and Westminster Hospital. Dr. Farthing has additional expertise in urogynecology and has published research in this field.

Bedford Close was a more private sort of residence and would actually have made a better place to murder someone. This suggested that the killer had Dando under surveillance and was closely following her movements. However, CCTV of Dando in her last minutes dredged up no evidence that anyone was following her by foot or by car. Jill Dando was murdered at 29 Gowan Avenue. This was a long street and the killer had to walk for a hundred metres in either direction after the shooting before there was any possibility of exiting the street. Not a great place to kill someone in broad daylight. The timing of the murder was - whether by design or accident - quite shrewd though because there were few people on the street that morning.

A possibility was that the killer lived in Fulham and so kept a close watch on Dando's comings and goings. If you lived in Fulham in the late 1990s you probably would have been aware that Jill Dando had a house in the area. You might even have seen her driving down the street or in a shop. There were reports of a smartly dressed man with a mobile phone 'stalking' Dando in the half-hour before her death. The police though could find no mobile phone records relating to this man in that location at this specific time. There is actually a theory that the mobile phone might have been ruse and that it was actually hollow and a place to hide the murder weapon.

A perspiring man was also reported to have jumped on a bus shortly after the murder but this man was never identified. It could have just been an innocent member of the public who had to run to catch his morning bus. The problem with the eyewitness statements in the Jill Dando case is that they were not consistent. They were all over the place. Some of these were unavoidably red herrings. The reliability of eyewitness statements can vary greatly depending on several factors. While eyewitness testimony has historically been considered strong evidence in legal proceedings, researchers have found that it is not always accurate or reliable. Memory decay and interference can also contribute to inaccuracies in eyewitness statements. Memories can fade over time or be altered by subsequent events. Similarly, if an eyewitness is exposed to other information or witnesses' statements, it can influence their memory and affect the accuracy of their statement.

The police had to sift through the eyewitness statements to see if they could find a pattern or anything which seemed especially pertinent and helpful. As we shall though it seems that the police essentially ignored what appeared to be the most salient eyewitness statement of all. Some reported seeing a Range Rover near Dando's home around the time the murder took place but - alas - this car could not be traced. The Range Rover was potentially highly suspicious because it was seen going through a red light. An eyewitness named Barry Lindsay, who we shall discuss later, had driven a Range Rover past Dando's home around the time of the murder but this was a different Range Rover. Was this Range Rover a getaway driver? That was certainly never proven.

The police came to believe the killer was a lone wolf who

had no accomplices and was a complete amateur (as opposed to a professional hitman or hardened criminal). That is basically the core division in the theories on this case. Jill Dando was either killed by a disturbed fan/stalker or she was killed in a professional hit. A popular theory was that Dando had been killed in revenge for a NATO attack on a TV station in Belgrade in which journalists were killed and injured. At the time of her death Jill Dando had recently fronted an appeal for Kosovan refugees. We shall discuss this theory later - though the police never appeared to show much interest in any of the Crimewatch/Belgrade theories. They certainly claim to have investigated these various competing theories but felt there was no evidence to take any of them seriously. The police 'experts' always seemed to believe the killer was a loner, a disturbed stalker who probably had some fixation with Jill Dando.

DCI Hamish Campbell was put in charge of the investigation to find Jill Dando's killer. The investigation to find Dando's killer was named Operation Oxborough. A veteran of the Metropolitan Police's criminal intelligence and anti-terrorist branches, Campbell joined the force in 1974. He was seen as a rising star in the Met but the Jill Dando case didn't do much for his reputation. Campbell must have felt like he'd got a poison chalice with the Dando case as there was intense pressure on the Met to find the killer.

The problem for the police was that were no obvious leads. You'd think that a shooting in west London in broad daylight would be fairly easy to solve but this obviously didn't turn out to be the case.

Campbell ultimately decided to put all of his eggs in the 'lone stalker' basket. All of the police profile experts said that the person who did this was most likely a member of the public with mental health issues. Campbell did not believe that this murder was carried out by professional criminals who were experienced in crimes like this. A man named Martyn Gilbert was an early police suspect. He was found to have discussed Jill Dando in rather grim sexually explicit terms in emails and also lived near to her in Fulham. He also moved to Australia two weeks after the murder - which could certainly be seen as suspicious. Detectives from the Met went to Australia to question Gilbert but then ruled him out as a suspect after these interviews so we must presume he had a cast iron alibi. Another suspect was a London mechanic named Steve Savva. Savva was actually put under police surveillance for six months before he was ruled out. The police had to investigate numerous men to whittle down the suspect list but at this point they were still whistling in the dark. They had no idea who had killed Jill Dando.

Jill Dando had visited a stationers and fishmongers before she made her way home to Fulham. She had purchased an ink cartridge for her fax machine and some Dover Sole for her dinner. CCTV in a Hammersmith shopping mall captured these last mundane fragments of her life. Dando then had a conversation with a traffic warden because she'd parked her BMW in the wrong place. The killer clearly seemed to anticipate that Dando was going to visit her Fulham home and moved in for the kill ruthlessly and efficiently - though the police might disagree because they didn't think the killer showed much professionalism at all in the murder.

The thing about hitmen or contract killers is that we've been conditioned to think of them through the prism of fiction. You tend to think that someone hired to murder someone for money must be some Jason Bourne type character. The reality is different though. Contract killers are human. They make mistakes. They shoot the wrong people. They sometimes give the impression of being not very professional. To this day there is no consensus on whether the person who shot Jill Dando was a professional criminal or a lone nutcase.

The killer bent Dando's head down as he shot her to ensure that only a single bullet would be needed and that she would fall quickly and out of sight. There was a bruise on Dando's arm from where the killer grabbed her. It was odd though that the killer had murdered Dando on her front path in broad daylight. Why not wait until she opened the door and follow her in? Maybe that chance never arose. Though she was found by neighbours and taken to hospital, Dando had no chance of surviving a bullet to the head at such close range and was officially pronounced dead not long after the incident. This was definitely one of the strangest true crime cases in recent years. A famous television presenter had been gunned down on her doorstep in a manner akin to a mob 'hit' on some poor Mafioso. It was all pretty bizarre and unbelievable.

* The music icon John Lennon was killed at the age of 40 by a disturbed fan named Mark Chapman. Chapman was a security guard with (no surprise here) mental health issues. He had contemplated suicide and become obsessed with John Lennon. He thought Lennon was a big hypocrite for singing songs about money not being important despite being a millionaire who lived a lavish lifestyle. Chapman bought a gun and flew to New York where Lennon lived with Yoko Ono. He staked out the Dakota Apartments building where Lennon resided and would often sign autographs outside as he came and went from the building. Chapman even got Lennon's autograph himself before he returned to kill the music icon. Chapman later said that Lennon had

been very nice and polite when he signed the autograph. That didn't stop him from shooting Lennon dead though.

When Yoko Ono and John Lennon returned to the Dakota at 10.50 pm, on Monday 8th December 1980, Chapman was waiting shot Lennon four times in the back. Less than half an hour later, Lennon was pronounced dead at the Roosevelt Hospital. Chapman did not flee the scene. He was detained by the Dakota's doorman until the police arrived. According to the autopsy report, two bullets entered the left side of Lennon's back, traveling through the left side of his chest and his left lung with one exiting from the body and one lodged in his neck. Two more bullets hit Lennon in his left shoulder. The chances of surviving these injuries were remote to say the least.

After he shot Lennon, Chapman apparently pulled out a copy of The Catcher in the Rye and started reading it. Inside his copy of The Catcher in the Rye, Chapman had written - "This is my statement", signing it "Holden Caulfield." Chapman was clearly a disturbed man. He had come to identify with Holden and viewed the world as being full of phonies. He claimed that he acted to preserve the 'innocence' of Lennon (which seems like a rather odd thing to say about a middle-aged millionaire musician who had known worldwide fame since the 1960s). Chapman felt Lennon had become a phoney. It came out during the court case that before the assassination Chapman would sit in his room chanting the mantra, "THE PHONY MUST DIE SAYS THE CATCHER IN THE RYE!"

Chapman changed his plea to guilty during the court case. His legal team had instructed him to enter a plea of not guilty by reason of insanity. The judge ordered psychiatric treatment for Chapman during his incarceration and sentenced him to twenty-years-to-life - five years less than the maximum sentence of twenty-five-years-to-life. Chapman has been denied parole eleven times and remains incarcerated in Wende Correctional Facility, east of Buffalo, New York. He has said that he regrets shooting John Lennon and shouldn't have done it but it's all a bit late now.

Christina Grimmie was a New Jersey born singer who first became famous and noticed after singing songs on YouTube. On the back of this she competed on the talent show The Voice (finishing in third place) and released an EP. Grimmie even launched an acting career by appearing in the 2016 independent film The Matchbreaker. She was famous for her high vocal range and an animal rights activist. Grimmie soon attracted famous friends and admirers and seemed like a very likeable and decent person. Christina Grimmie seemed set for a very promising career and even picked up a Teen Choice Award for her music. Fate was to intervene though in shocking fashion.

On June 10, 2016, Grimmie performed a show in Orlando and signed some autographs for fans in the arena after the concert. Grimmie was very generous in taking time out to talk to fans and sign autographs and she enjoyed this fan interaction because being famous was still relatively new to her and so it was all rather novel and flattering. She was just a nice person who was happy to meet new people and thank anyone who supported her music career by coming out to watch her sing and perform.

At one point during her autograph signing session, Grimmie innocently moved forward to hug a fan who appeared to be moving in for an autograph. At this moment, to the absolute horror of everyone, the fan produced a gun and shot her multiple times. The disturbed fan was a 27 year-old man named Kevin James Loibl. Grimmie's brother managed to wrestle Loibl to the ground but he then broke free and shot himself dead. Christina Grimmie's own injuries were - sadly - fatal. She had been shot four times. A food vendor at the arena later said he heard four or five quick shots and saw Grimmie lying on the floor covered in blood. It was a horrifying scene.

Although she was taken to hospital Christina Grimmie was pronounced dead about thirty minutes after the fatal shooting took place. She was just twenty-two years-old. Kevin James Loibl had travelled to Orlando for the concert from his home in St. Petersburg, Florida. In his bag that night he had two guns, ammunition, and a hunting knife. The police believed he had developed a romantic obsession with Christina Grimmie and decided that if he couldn't have her then no one else would. The family of Loibl said they had no idea he was even a fan of Christina Grimmie - let alone had plans to kill her.

There was some criticism of the arena security that night because although they were supposed to search people going in the searches hadn't been that thorough because Loibl was able to walk in with two guns and a knife. In fairness to the staff they obviously could have no way of knowing that a disturbed fan was planning to kill Christina that night. What might have prevented the tragedy was metal detectors as people went in but sadly no such provision had been made that night. The arena staff obviously presumed that Christina's fans were harmless kids just out to have a good time - and all but one were. Thousands of fans attended the memorial service for Christina Grimmie. A bright young life had been wiped out in the most harrowing and unexpected fashion.

Selena Quintanilla-Pérez was a Texas born Latino singer who became a huge star in the 1990s. She was hugely popular and famous for her impressive vocal range. She won numerous awards, had great commercial success, and signed with a major label. Selena was known as the queen of Tejano. Fate was intervene in tragic fashion though thanks to Yolanda Saldívar. Yolanda Saldívar was a fomer nurse who became obsessed with Selena after attending one of her concerts. Saldívar began badgering Selena's father (who was obviously someone with great influence over his daughter's career and business empire) with requests for permission to start a Selena fan club in San Antonio. Permission for this was eventually granted and Yolanda Saldívar turned the regional fan club into a great success, attracting thousands of members.

As a reward for her efforts, Yolanda Saldívar was taken into the Selena business empire and became her local agent. Saldívar was then put in charge of the chain of fashion boutiques Selena had opened. Though no one knew it at the time it was a huge and eventually tragic mistake to allow Yolanda Saldívar to become part of team Selena. Yolanda Saldívar even moved house to be closer to Selena. Trouble was brewing though because there were soon rumblings of discontent from others in Selena's entourage about Yolanda Saldívar. They simply didn't like Saldívar and they didn't trust her either. This sixth sense turned to be completely on the mark. Yolanda Saldívar, to put it mildly, was bad news and seriously unhinged.

It soon transpired that Yolanda Saldívar had a habit of firing staff members she didn't like in the Selena boutiques - which began to have an effect on sales. Saldívar had grown to enjoy the power she had and was throwing her weight around at every opportunity. Other members of Selena's inner circle grew to dislike Yolanda Saldívar and wanted to get rid of her. Selena's father was among those who wanted to give Saldívar the boot in the end. Selena stood by Yolanda Saldívar out of loyalty but matters came to a head when it was discovered that Saldívar had embezzled thousands of dollars from the boutiques and fan club.

Yolanda Saldívar is said to have stolen about $60,000 through her duties as boutique manager and boss of the Selena fan club. The crimes became apparent when people started writing in and complaining that they had sent their money to join the Selena fan club but received nothing in return. Unknown to Selena and her family, Yolanda Saldívar had previous when it came to dodgy and criminal deeds. In 1984 she had stolen $9000 from a doctor she worked as a book-keeper for. Saldívar had settled the case out of court and obviously managed to keep this hidden when she was employed by Selena.

On March 31, 1995, in Corpus Christi, Texas, Selena arranged to meet Saldívar at a motel and confronted her with the financial fraud charges. Selana demanded to see financial documents whereupon Yolanda Saldívar produced a handgun and pointed it at Selana. Selena tried to flee but was shot in the back. The bullet severed an artery and exited through Selena's chest. Saldívar then chased the injured Selena down a corridor shouting abuse. Motel staff arrived on the scene and Selena, who was seriously injured and covered in blood, managed to give them Saldívar's name and room number before she passed out.

Though an ambulance only took two minutes to arrive it was already too late because Selena had lost so much blood. Selena collapsed and died in hospital shortly afterwards of blood loss and cardiac arrest. She was only 23 years-old. The doctors said that if the bullet had entered Selena's body a tiniest fraction to either side she probably would have survived. Tragically though the single bullet went in at a crucial spot and caused too much damage.

Yolanda Saldívar tried to get in her car and drive away but after a nine hour stand-off she was captured by police officers and FBI agents. Saldívar sat in the car for hours threatening to shoot herself. Yolanda Saldívar's legal team tried to claim the murder of Selena had been an accident but this didn't stand up to much scrutiny in court. The prosecution pointed out that Yolanda Saldívar was a trained nurse yet made no attempt to offer medical assistance to the wounded Selena - thus confirming that the murder was intentional.

CHAPTER TWO

The first thing the police have to do in unsolved murder cases like that of Jill Dando is investigate the family and friends of the victim. A surprising number of people are killed by someone they already know. There were nearly 500 names in Dando's Filofax (a binder wallet which people used to use to store contacts) and the police had to check all of these people out. This was a painstaking and laborious task and it proved to be a dead end. There was nothing in Dando's private life which gave any clue as to why she might have been killed. She had no enemies and there were no grudges or feuds in her past. Her friends and family were ruled out as suspects - as too was the man she was set to marry and her ex-boyfriends. There was actually a weird tabloid story about Dando years later in which it was said that, when she was alive, someone had pretended to be her brother and tried to get her energy bill arrangements changed. This story was never really clarified but it was certainly interesting. Was this person a deranged fan? A criminal trying to get information on Dando? A journalist?

Dando was due to get married and seemed well liked by everyone who had crossed her path. There was no spurned lover to investigate - nor indeed even a 'Dando stalker' on any police files. Well, that's not completely true. Jill Dando did actually have a problem with a stalker in 1998. The man in question was John Hole - a retired civil servant from Kent. Hole sent letters and Valentine cards to Dando and kept turning up at the BBC television centre trying to meet her. He rang the BBC a lot too asking to talk to her. In the end Dando wrote to John Hole and asked him to leave her alone. John Hole was generally considered to be more of an eccentric pest than a dangerous person and was certainly not a suspect in Dando's murder. Hole actually used to talk to the media and told them he thought that Jill Dando was a lovely person who he just wanted to meet. The chances of this ever happening had been precisely zero. Hole lived with his mother until her death. He was never married.

The police investigating the murder came around to the idea that the person who killed Dando was some lone wolf stalker who had yet to enter their radar. They believed if they could find a man who most matched their expert profiles (on the type of person most likely to have done this) in the immediate area then that was more than likely the killer of Jill Dando. Offender profiles, also known as criminal profiles or psychological profiles, are a tool used to help identify and apprehend criminals. These profiles are created based on a combination of known information, evidence, and behavioural traits exhibited by the offender.

While it is important to note that offender profiles are not foolproof and can vary in accuracy, they can provide valuable insights into the mindset and characteristics of the individual responsible for a crime. Demographics can sometimes provide helpful context in understanding motive or determining potential targets. The modus operandi (MO) refers to the specific methods or tactics that the offender uses to commit a crime. This includes details such as the time, location, weapons, entry/exit points, and any distinctive patterns or rituals the offender may exhibit in their crimes. The signature behavior is distinct from the MO and refers to unique aspects of the crime that have no practical function but are instead driven by the offender's psychological needs or desires. It can include factors such as the use of specific symbols, leaving messages or signatures at the crime scene, or engaging in specific patterns of violence.

If the offender has a previous criminal record, it can provide insight into their history, past offenses, and potential escalation of criminal behaviour. Understanding the underlying motivations of an offender can assist in identifying potential triggers or patterns in their crimes. Motivations can vary widely, such as financial gain, power and control, sexual gratification, revenge, or thrill-seeking. Offender files also delve into the offender's psychological and behavioural characteristics. It may include traits such as their intelligence level, social skills, personality disorders, mental health issues, and possible motives for the crimes committed.

The study of victimology helps to identify patterns in the choice of victims, including age, gender, occupation, and relationships to the offender. This can assist in narrowing down potential suspects or establishing a link between different crimes. It is essential to note that offender profiles are not infallible. They are based on the understanding that certain behaviours tend to correlate with certain personality traits or motivations. Each case and offender is unique, and profiles can evolve or be refined as more information becomes available.

A team of 45 detectives were assigned to the Jill Dando investigation. One of their tasks was to sift through thousands of emails sent to the BBC in the hope that one of these might yield an important clue. Once again though the police drew a frustrating blank. It later transpired that the BBC received some 'threatening' calls in relation to the NATO bombing of the Serbian television headquarters but this is evidently not something that the police felt was of any consequence in relation to the Jill Dando case.

The police focus was on the 'lone madman stalker' theory. They believed the killer was almost certainly some disturbed local obsessive loner who had an obsession with Jill Dando. Given the seemingly professional and efficient nature of the murder the police theory was highly questionable. The killer had managed to murder one of the most famous people in Britain in broad daylight and then vanish in London streets. The killer was therefore either incredibly elusive and shrewd or incredibly lucky. Either way it seemed to be someone who knew this area well - be that through planning or actually living in Fulham.

The police collected a list of around 2,000 suspects. Many of these were people who had complaints against them by women, criminal convictions for sexual offences, and a history of stalking. The police then narrowed this down to 148 people who they believed had displayed a specific interest in Jill Dando (though how you quantify an 'interest' in Jill Dando is anyone's guess). Using the TIE system the police set about investigating the people on this list. TIE is an acronym that stands for Trace, Interview, and Eliminate. It is an investigative process commonly used in law enforcement and criminal investigations. Trace: The first step in the TIE process involves tracing relevant information or evidence.

Investigators gather all available data and evidence related to the case, such as witness statements, physical evidence, phone records, surveillance footage, and any other relevant documents or information. This step is crucial as it helps establish a starting point and potential leads for further investigation. Interview: The second step is to conduct interviews with individuals who may have information relevant to the case. This includes witnesses, victims, suspects, and anyone else who could provide relevant details or insights. Investigators utilize their questioning and interpersonal skills to gather as much information as possible. Interviews help provide clues, establish motives, and eliminate potential suspects.

Eliminate: The final step is to eliminate potential suspects based on the evidence and information gathered during the tracing and interviewing stages. By analysing the available data and comparing it with the facts of the case, investigators can exclude individuals who do not match the profile of the perpetrator. This step helps narrow down the list of potential suspects, focusing resources on those who are most likely to be involved. Overall, TIE is a systematic approach that helps investigators gather relevant information, interview key individuals, and eliminate potential suspects. It is an effective method for progressing investigations, identifying the truth, and bringing justice to victims and their families.

Despite the 2,000 suspects they began with the police only had eyes for one in the end. A certain Barry George. At least one person was arrested before Barry George but he was released without charge. Barry George was born in Hammersmith in 1960 and lived in a basement flat about 500 yards from where Jill Dando's home in Fulham was. He'd had a difficult childhood and went to special schools. George was not what you would describe as the sharpest knife in the drawer. He was unemployed and what you could describe as a local oddball. The police obsession with this man was puzzling in many ways - especially in hindsight now that we know what happened in the years to come. Barry George does tend to divide opinion though on this case. The majority view is that George was always innocent of the murder. Others though have never let go of the belief that he was guilty.

Once they had become aware of Barry George, the police simply refused to accept that anyone other than him could be responsible for the murder of Jill Dando. The evidence for adopting this stubborn stance though was not exactly conclusive or overwhelming and this made the police fixation on Barry George questionable to say the least. It is certainly understandable though why George became a figure of interest to the police investigation. He was deeply weird with a dark past. He ticked a number of boxes (especially if one was minded to go down the lone stalker route). Barry George also lived within walking distance of Jill Dando's old home in Fulham. He was definitely someone you would want to talk to and maybe eliminate or question more. The concrete evidence for him being the killer of Jill Dando was always elusive though. It was always slightly beyond the grasp of the police. The case against Barry George was simply never as strong as the Met wanted it to be.

Barry George was a loner with learning difficulties. He was certainly an odd character but being eccentric does not automatically make one a murderer. If we were to allow the police to arrest all eccentric people purely for being eccentric then half the nation's population would end up behind bars. Most of us are eccentric in our own different ways. To put it in crude and politically incorrect terms, many felt that the police in this investigation simply decided to 'stitch-up the local nutter' rather than fully explore other possibilities. As we shall see though, the police felt this was a gross and inaccurate simplification of the investigation. They spent a year investigating all possibilities before the name Barry George even landed on their desk.

One might argue though with some justification that the police were too far short-sighted in this case and too obsessed with making Barry George fit the murder - as opposed to making the murder fit Barry George. Others though would disagree. Indeed, there are still people today (including Hamish Campbell and Nick Ross) who seem to believe Barry George was the killer. One obvious problem with the theory that Barry George was the person who efficiently murdered Jill Dando and then evaded capture by vanishing is that he seemed for all the world like someone suffering from neurological damage. His speech was slow and slurred like a punch drunk boxer and he wasn't exactly the most athletic person. He had a rather shambling gait and was famously useless at everyday tasks. Was this person really capable of planning a murder and then successfully carrying it out?

Barry George often went by the name Barry Bulsara (Bulsara was the real second name of Barry George's hero Freddie Mercury). George would often pretend he was Freddie Mercury's cousin. You would have to be very gullible to have believed this - which probably explains why George would apparently run this ruse out on Japanese tourists. Some of those in the Queen fandom community complained about Barry George and said he was a pest. This was merely the tip of the iceberg when it came to his pseudonyms. George had once changed his name to Steve Majors (this name appeared to be a mash-up of the actor Lee Majors and his 'bionic man' character Steve Austin) and pretended to be a stuntman. In other circumstances, Barry George's life story would have been funny and worthy of a comedy film. Other parts of his life were too dark though to make him a sympathetic character.

George had broken bones once attempting a roller-skate stunt jumping over Double Decker buses as his Steve Majors alter-ego. A video of this is available online. George is surprisingly youthful and articulate in an interview before the stunt. A long way removed from the monosyllabic drunken sounding Barry George of 1999. Barry George roller skated down a ramp and managed to get over about two and a half buses before he (predictably) clattered into one and came a cropper. No sane person would have attempted this stunt but Barry George seemed desperate for some degree of attention or fame. He was a man who just wanted the world to notice he was there.

Barry George adopted various eccentric and bizarre aliases in his life. He once went by the name of Paul Gadd (the real name of the disgraced pop star Gary Glitter). He once even made a court appearance dressed as Gary Glitter. Barry George lived in what you might describe as a fantasy world of his own. When he was younger he once got into trouble for pretending to be a police officer. George had made a fake police ID card and pretended he was a plain clothes detective. This happened after he had tried to join the police for real but had been rejected. George also falsely claimed to be the British Karate Champion. He had these various fake characters he would create and then assume the identity of. Barry George was plainly someone who didn't like being himself very much.

George was like a low IQ cross between Aldridge Prior (the hopeless liar) from Viz and Walter Mitty. Walter Mitty is the main character in James Thurber's short story "The Secret Life of Walter Mitty," which was first published in 1939. Walter Mitty is a middle-aged man who leads a dull and monotonous life as a henpecked husband in real life. However, in his vivid imagination, he embarks on exciting and elaborate daydreams in which he becomes a heroic figure involved in adventurous situations.

In each daydream, Walter Mitty takes on a different role, such as a brave pilot, a skilled surgeon, or a fearless war hero. These fantasies allow him to escape the banalities of his everyday life and experience a sense of excitement and fulfilment. However, Walter's daydreaming often leads to comical and awkward situations in reality, as he loses touch with his surroundings and fails to complete ordinary tasks. Through the character of Walter Mitty, Thurber explores themes of escapism, the monotony of modern life, and the power of imagination. Mitty's daydreams are a manifestation of his desire for adventure and significance, reflecting the dissatisfaction he feels with his ordinary existence.

Barry George was judged to have Asperger syndrome and various personality disorders. And yet the police made no accommodation to these issues. They treated him as if he was a normal person. Asperger syndrome, also known as Asperger's or high-functioning autism, is a neurodevelopmental disorder characterised by significant difficulties in social interaction and nonverbal communication, as well as restricted and repetitive patterns of behaviour and interests. It is considered to be on the autism spectrum and is often diagnosed in early childhood.

People with Asperger syndrome typically have difficulty understanding and interpreting social cues, such as body language, facial expressions, and tone of voice. This can lead to challenges in making and maintaining friendships, as well as problems with social interactions in general. They may have a tendency to engage in one-sided conversations, talk at length about their specific interests, or struggle with taking turns during conversations. As a result, individuals with Asperger syndrome may be perceived as socially awkward or insensitive.

In addition to difficulties in social interactions, individuals with Asperger syndrome often display repetitive and restricted patterns of behaviour and interests. They may develop intense interests in certain topics, often to the exclusion of other activities. These interests may be highly detailed and specific, and individuals may spend a significant amount of time collecting information and learning about their chosen subject. They may also engage in repetitive behaviours, such as hand-flapping or rocking, as a way to self-soothe or regulate sensory input.

It is important to note that individuals with Asperger syndrome often have average to above-average intelligence, and may excel in areas that are related to their specific interests. However, they may struggle with abstract thinking, executive functioning skills, and understanding the perspectives of others. Although there is no cure for Asperger syndrome, early intervention and support can greatly improve an individual's quality of life. This may include social skills training, occupational therapy, speech therapy, and educational supports. With the right interventions, individuals with Asperger syndrome can learn strategies to improve their social interactions and daily functioning.

Barry George would also pretend he managed rock bands and hand out business cards for fictitious companies he claimed to own. in reality he had nothing. No job and no money. Women had no interest in him either. This all made Barry George feel helpless and frustrated. He retreated more and more into a fantasy world. Barry George was, to put it bluntly, barking mad. But was he capable of murder? The police had Barry George under surveillance for nearly a year before they arrested him. They were certainly under pressure to solve the case and in Barry George they believed they had finally made a breakthrough. The police never wavered on this even when the evidence didn't always prove as conclusive as they might have hoped. They never deviated from the belief that Barry George was the prime suspect.

The police said that Barry George was not someone, contrary to popular opinion, they zeroed in on as a convenient local scapegoat but rather someone who had been suggested to them several times by the local community in Fulham as a potential suspect. A number of people called the police after Dando's murder and suggested the Met should check out this local 'oddball' in Fulham who gave them an uneasy feeling and was known to be something of a pest when it came to women. The police decided they had to check out this Barry George character for themselves and once they did they found him to be highly suspicious.

The police believed that George was a perfect match for the offender file they had constructed to paint a picture of who might have done this baffling murder. Barry George fitted the 'lone stalker' profile they favoured and lived very close to where Jill Dando had been shot. There is no doubt that Barry George knew those streets very well.

The police were absolutely determined to convict Barry George - to the point where one might argue that they adopted too narrow a vision of this case and did not fully explore other credible theories and lines of enquiry. Far too much stock was put in the offender file. Was the police interest in Barry George justified or was it a big mistake? Well, as we have noted, to this day opinions on that differ. The general view though is that this was a miscarriage of justice. Many experts believe the police were barking up the wrong tree.

The police (rather ludicrously) noted that Barry George was found to have several newspapers containing articles about Jill Dando in his grotty flat at 2b Crookham Road. Given that George was a mentally troubled hoarder with hundreds of newspapers and magazines in his flat it would have been nigh on impossible for none of these newspapers to mention Jill Dando because she was one of the most famous people in the country at the time they were published. Millions of people in 1999 probably had an old newspaper or magazine containing an article about Jill Dando lying around in their house. This police evidence proved absolutely nothing. It wasn't evidence at all. In fact it should have been deemed counter-productive to the case against Barry George because according to the offender profile the man they were looking for was supposed to be obsessed with Jill Dando.

There was never any proof in the investigation that Barry

George had any particular interest in Jill Dando. There were no pictures of her on the wall in his flat. There was no Jill Dando scrapbook. No videos of her taped off the television. No pictures of her cut out of newspapers. There was though a shrine in the flat to Freddie Mercury. One very odd thing the police did notice was that Barry George had blurry photographs of female celebrities he would take off the television. Jill Dando though was not a feature of this at all. Despite the lack of evidence in relation to their main suspect, the police theory was obviously that George had become obsessed with Jill Dando and begun stalking her. This is sadly something that does happen - especially to female celebrities.

Given that Dando was engaged and due to be married you can see how the police probably came up with a scenario where George had been angered and upset by this engagement and decided that if he couldn't have Jill Dando then no one would. The police said that George was found to have four copies of the BBC in-house magazine Ariel memorial to Jill Dando in his flat but it's hard to see how this evidence could be used against him. Many people kept newspaper memorials after the death of Princess Diana but it doesn't mean they killed her! Besides, Barry George used to work as a runner at the BBC and it was there (years before Dando was famous) that he started collecting Ariel magazine. The five month job as a runner in the late 1970s was the only time Barry George had worked in his entire life. He had no qualifications and was basically unemployable.

The police believed that, at some point or other, Barry George had met Jill Dando (perhaps he had got her autograph in the street or something?) and become infatuated. This was certainly never verified though. It seems possible though that he might have seen her from afar in the street in Fulham. The police found a note in George's flat in which he confessed that he had trouble dealing with rejection and that this made him angry. They believed that this 'confession' was applicable to his attitude towards Jill Dando. Once again though it was more of a theory or hunch than something which had been proven. The specific note in question did not make any reference to Jill Dando by name. George could have been talking about anyone (he was once involved in a marriage that collapsed) or just his feelings in general. Barry George was the sort of person that women would cross the street to avoid and he was aware of this. It was painful for him and left him feeling sad and frustrated. Was it enough though to turn him into a killer?

CHAPTER THREE

The biggest problem with the police case against Barry George for many is that the murder was - on the face of it at least - highly efficient and seemed to be meticulously planned in advance. It was done very quickly (the bullet was shot into Dando's temple) and the killer was very elusive in rapidly escaping from the crime scene without much detection at all. This all suggested that the killer was reasonably fast on his feet and athletic, had maybe done this sort of thing before, and was of above average intelligence. Barry George, by contrast, was an overweight shambles of a man who could barely tie his own shoelaces. It beggared belief to think that he would have been capable of this stealth Mafia style assassination. Was that an unfair assessment though? There were certainly other views available and Hamish Campbell was decidedly not of the opinion that one needed to have been James Bond to carry out this murder. This was the basic crux of the case. Was the killer a hitman or a stalker? A professional or an amateur?

Jill Dando was killed with a 9mm Short calibre semi-automatic pistol. The cartridge was judged to have been modified in a workshop to make the gun less noisy (some of the neighbours of Jill Dando heard her scream but not all of them said they heard a gun being fired). This was an important detail in the case because the police believe that a professional hitman would not have used such a crude weapon. A weapon of this makeshift type ran a very real risk of jamming or falling apart. This made the police believe an 'amateur' was involved - thus (in the police view) solidifying their belief that Barry George was the killer. Like so much in the case against Barry George though this was all highly debatable.

One possible problem with this theory was that it implied that Barry George (who was plainly no Einstein) was capable of modifying a firearm in a workshop - or indeed had the connections to arrange for this to be done. Both of these assumptions seemed very questionable. As a police officer (who obviously didn't think George was the killer) later pointed out, Barry George didn't even know how to fit a light on his bike. Was this man really capable of creating a gun and ammunition in a workshop for a murder? The modifications on the gun were obviously successful too. The gun had worked. It wasn't as if the gun fell to pieces or failed to go off.

The police argued though that Barry George's old school had a small-bore rifle range which he would probably have become familiar with. They also pointed out that George had briefly served with the Territorial Army and attended the Kensington and Chelsea gun club for a few sessions in the early eighties (though George was unsuccessful when he applied for full membership of this club). Once again though none of this evidence seemed completely convincing. Barry George was not a stranger to guns but he certainly wasn't an expert either. That would be like presuming that someone who had an air rifle when they were a kid was therefore a gun expert as an adult. It doesn't work like that. Barry George spent 29 days in the Territorial Army and did no pistol or gun training at all in that time.

The police noted, with great interest, that Barry George's flat was full of gun magazines. Barry George was the sort of person who had balaclavas, gas masks, and fake replica guns in his flat. He would take photographs of himself with these and pretend he was in the elite special forces unit called the SAS. One of George's common pseudonyms was Tom Palmer - one of the SAS soldiers who foiled the 1980 Iranian Embassy Siege. The 1980 Iranian Embassy Siege, also known as Operation Nimrod, was a hostage crisis that took place in London. The incident occurred on April 30, 1980 when six gunmen stormed the Iranian embassy in South Kensington, taking 26 people hostage. The gunmen were members of an Arab separatist group called the Democratic Revolutionary Front for the Liberation of Arabistan (DRFLA), who demanded the release of prisoners from Khuzestan Province in Iran. They also expressed their support for the Iranian opposition group, the People's Mujahedin of Iran (MEK).

Over the course of the six-day siege, negotiations broke down, leading the gunmen to kill one of the hostages and throw his body out of the embassy. This act hardened the resolve of Margaret Thatcher to end the crisis by force if necessary. On May 5, 1980, Operation Nimrod was launched. The Special Air Service (SAS) stormed the embassy. In a carefully executed operation, the SAS quickly overwhelmed the gunmen and rescued the remaining hostages. Five of the six terrorists were killed, while one was captured. This incident made the SAS world famous and saw applications to join them go through the roof. The SAS men were seen entering the embassy on live TV in their distinctive black uniforms, hoods, and gas masks. The incident inspired the 1982 Lewis Collins action film Who Dares Wins. Barry George was greatly excited by all of this. He assembled his own SAS outfit in his flat and fantasised of being in the Special Air Service. He was a daydreamer who couldn't live in the real world.

To state the obvious, Barry George was not the full shilling. This is not someone that you would want to live next door to. There was no conclusive evidence that he was a murderer though. Barry George was just a strange man with learning difficulties. He patently needed more care and supervision. Barry George's evidence was all over the place in police interviews. He was predictably all at sea trying to defend himself from accusations that he was a killer. He never showed any emotion either - which didn't help his case.

The police took him to be a cold hearted killer with no remorse or human emotions but Barry George was simply a blank. He was a tabula rasa. If you told Barry George the world was about to end he would probably look at you with a blank face and hardly register this news. The lack of emotion was a red flag to the police.

In his dealings with the police, Barry George gave no great indication that he even knew what was happening to him or that he was aware he was in big trouble. He was generally in a world of his own. When he was questioned by the police in relation to Jill Dando's murder it is doubtful that George even grasped the gravity of the situation he was in. There is evidence, as we shall see, though that George had gone to some lengths to establish an alibi. He said he had not done this because he was guilty but simply because he knew the police were probably going to talk to him about the murder at some point. Barry George had anticipated this not only because he lived in Fulham near where Dando was murdered but also because of his grim history when it came to women.

Barry George was no angel. The police found evidence that he was something of a stalkerish sex pest and sometimes followed women on the street. Some women reported that George had come up to them on the street and suddenly kissed them - whereupon they had to fight him off and run away. Barry George had been arrested for indecent assault in the past but these cases did not go to court. In 1982 though he served some time in prison for attempted rape (George had pled not guilty to the charge). The police and prosecution in the Jill Dando managed to find a number of women who said they'd had a creepy encounter with Barry George where he'd followed them or simply started talking to them and bothering them on the street.

It turned out that Barry George had been spoken to the police several times in the 1980s for groping and harassing women. In one incident he had allegedly attacked a young languages student in Acton. Barry George seemed to have no understanding of boundaries and personal space. He was socially inept. The police found 418 photographs in Barry George's flat of women he had secretly photographed in the street. He had also written down the car registrations of a number of women. All the evidence for Barry George's peeping Tomdom and creepy harassment of women was ruled inadmissible in the first trial. The prosecution (and doubtless the police too) were understandably rather annoyed about this. They believed it would have greatly strengthened their case against him. In this though they were (surprisingly perhaps) to be proved wrong. When this evidence was allowed in the second trial it didn't really make much difference to the case.

After he was arrested, 43 women in Fulham told the police they had experienced a sexual harassment incident involving Barry George. He was clearly a troubled and unsavoury character. There was no doubt about that. The key question now though was this - was Barry George a killer? Had he killed Jill Dando? The doctors who assessed Barry George for the trial judged him to have psychopathic personality characteristics. Those suffering from this condition are prone to impulsivity and irrational behaviour. Individuals with psychopathic tendencies often exhibit impulsive and reckless behaviour. They make hasty decisions without considering the long-term consequences, acting purely on their immediate desires and emotions. This impulsivity makes them prone to engage in criminal activities.

One could certainly see indications of impulsivity and irrational behaviour in Barry George but it is open to question if he displayed the full panoply of characteristics commonly connected to a psychopathic personality. The superficial charm usually associated with a psychopathic personality was nowhere to be found in Barry George and he certainly didn't display a grandiose narcissism. As for a lack of empathy, well, we simply don't know. Only Barry George would really know if he had regret and remorse for the things he had done. It was certainly a stretch to say that Barry George might be a psychopath. There was no evidence that he'd ever tried to kill anyone or was consistently violent. He was more of a creepy oddball than a potential serial killer.

In 1983, Barry George had been found lurking in the grounds of Kensington Palace where Charles and Diana lived. George was wearing wearing khaki and had a knife and some rope. When he was apprehended by the police, Barry George could supply no explanation of what he had been doing there. The police profile on Barry George for the Jill Dando case asserted that his aim that night was to break in and find or harm Princess Diana. That was certainly a questionable assertion. It could be the case that George was acting out of his SAS fantasies and had no idea that it would be construed as if he was out to harm Diana. Barry George was a walking example of the tension between fantasy and reality. We all have to live in reality. We have no choice about that - however disappointing reality might often be. Barry George didn't understand this though. He lived in a fantasy world of his own making and this constantly got him into trouble in the REAL world.

Barry George had been found on these royal grounds more than once and was on a police list of people who might potentially pose a danger to the royal family. Barry George was also said to have stayed up all night to get a prime spot near Westminster Abbey for Princess Diana's funeral. The police theory was that George had been obsessed with Diana and after her death had transferred this obsession over to Jill Dando. Diana and Jill Dando, who were about the same age, both had the same sort of hairstyle and were not entirely dissimilar. There was though never much evidence for the theory that Barry George was obsessed with Jill Dando. * This was certainly a weakness in the police case in that it was more of a theory than anything which had been proved but it didn't seem to bother the Met too much and they continued to pursue the case as if this fact was somehow incontrovertible.

The tabloids later managed to track down a Japanese woman named Itsuko Toide. Itsuko Toide had briefly been married to Barry George in what was describe as a marriage of convenience designed to allow Toide to stay in the country (although she later went back to Japan anyway). They married in a low-key ceremony at Fulham Register Office on May 2, 1989. The relatives of Barry George mostly stayed away from the wedding service because he had been disowned after his rape conviction. Itsuko Toide said she hadn't known about Barry George's dark past. Toide described life with Barry George as awful. She said that she refused to have sexual relations with Barry George and in the end he tried to rape her. She fled from their flat after six months and never went back.

Itsuko Toide later told the newspapers though that during the doomed marriage she had seen no evidence whatsoever that Barry George had any particular interest in Princess Diana or Jill Dando. Given that she had lived with Barry George it seems reasonable to think that she would know a lot more about this than a police officer compiling an offender profile in an office. Itsuko Toide did not believe either that Barry George had murdered Jill Dando. Though she clearly had no love for her former husband she did not believe he would have been capable of that. Itsuko Toide did not tell any of this to the Met though. When detectives from London tried to contact her to talk about Barry George she refused to meet with them. Itsuko Toide said she just wanted to forget about Barry George.

* When they searched Barry George's flat the police found that George had some pictures of the television presenter Anthea Turner which had been set to one side. There was nothing like this relating to Jill Dando though. If it was Anthea Turner who had been murdered the police would

have had a somewhat stronger case in insisting that Barry George had a fixation on her!

CHAPTER FOUR

One of the reasons why the police were convinced of the 'lone wolf stalker' theory is that they'd drawn a blank when it came to their network of police informants. The police believed that if this was a Crimewatch related hit they would have heard something about it by now from their contacts in the criminal underworld. The police believed that a gangster or hitman who had murdered Jill Dando wouldn't be able to resist boasting about this to someone or other and they would consequently have heard some whispers to this effect. The Met's police informants and underworld grapevine maintained a deafening radio silence though on this specific front. As for the Serbian theory, the police felt they had not had any contact from the intelligence community with information that made this compelling. This is why their focus had eventually fallen on Barry George.

The police had a theory that Barry George was suffering from De Clerambault's syndrome - a psychiatric syndrome characterised by the delusional belief that one is loved by another person of, generally of a higher social status. This belief is usually maintained despite the lack of any evidence or reciprocation from the object of their delusion.

Individuals with De Clerambault's syndrome may develop obsessive thoughts about the person they believe is in love with them and may interpret harmless actions or gestures as proof of this love. They may also engage in persistent, unwanted communication or stalking behaviours in an attempt to establish a relationship with the person they have delusions about.

This syndrome often occurs in the context of other psychiatric disorders, such as schizophrenia or bipolar disorder, and may be associated with other delusional beliefs or paranoid ideation. The exact cause of De Clerambault's syndrome is still unknown, but it is believed to be a combination of biological factors, such as genetic or neurochemical abnormalities, and psychological or environmental factors. Treatment for De Clerambault's syndrome typically involves a combination of psychotherapy and medication. Cognitive-behavioral therapy can help individuals challenge their delusional beliefs and develop healthier coping mechanisms. Antipsychotic medications may also be prescribed to manage any associated psychotic symptoms or underlying psychiatric conditions. However, the prognosis for De Clerambault's syndrome is generally considered to be poor, as the delusions often persist despite treatment efforts.

The problem with this theory though is that, as Itsuko Toide later noted, Barry George never displayed any interest (let alone an obsession) in Jill Dando. The belief that Barry George was obsessed with Jill Dando was basically just a police hunch or theory rather than anything backed up with hard evidence. There were only a handful of photographs of Jill Dando in the many newspapers and magazines found in Barry George's flat and not a single one of these had been cut out. There were plenty of people in Fulham who said George talked at length about Jill Dando and her murder after the tragedy but none of them recalled him ever mentioning her at all when she was alive. Barry George was always desperate for attention so the fact that a celebrity had been murdered on his doorstep (so to speak) naturally brought him out of his flat to talk to strangers about this strange crime and somehow insert himself into the little hub of media and public activity now going on in the aftermath.

The police were patently convinced that this case was analogous to something like the murder of Rebecca Schaeffer in Hollywood a decade before. They clearly believed that this was a celebrity stalker murder and that Barry George was their man. Rebecca Schaeffer was a twenty-one year-old actress in 1989 and starring in the popular CBS sitcom My Sister Sam. Schaeffer was also up for a part in The Godfather III and had appeared in Woody Allen's Radio Days. She seemed destined to use her sitcom fame as a springboard to a movie career - and had even made tentative early steps towards this goal. Schaeffer was an attractive curly haired brunette who once had aspirations to be a model. Though she found that she wasn't tall enough to be a model her talent as an actor more than compensated and her career in Hollywood was highly promising. Schaeffer was intelligent and ambitious and loved by her family and friends.

Rebecca Schaeffer resided in the Fairfax District of Los Angeles and had an apartment in a Mock Tudor house. Although she was making good money from her sitcom she was a fairly down to earth person and wasn't living an extravagant Hollywood life. Schaeffer was more interested in her career and work than fame but tragically it was her fame that would lead to her premature death. One day, Schaeffer heard her doorbell and rushed down thinking it was a script she was expecting to be delivered that morning. Instead she found a young man outside the house who turned out to be a fan who had tracked her down. The intercom didn't work so Rebecca had no choice but to go down and see who wanted to talk to her.

The young man was 19 year-old Robert John Bardo. Bardo was from Tuscon and had become obsessed with Schaeffer after watching her in My Sister Sam. He had previously written her a fan letter and she had penned a polite response with 'love Rebecca' at the end. She did this with all fan letters but Bardo, who was clearly not the full shilling, read way more than was intended into this and assumed he now had some sort of special relationship with Schaeffer that no other fan shared.

Bardo was definitely a bit creepy but Schaeffer didn't sense any danger from him when she opened the door. It was probably Bardo's youth that mitigated any sense of threat. He was still a teenager and even younger than she was. Schaeffer signed an autograph for Bardo and then - as politely as she could - cut short the small talk and went back up to her apartment. Bardo left the neighbourhood but he didn't go home. He went to a nearby diner and had some cheesecake. Bardo was simmering with anger because he felt Schaeffer had been indifferent to him and simply got rid of him as fast as she could. He'd long harboured a delusional fantasy that Rebecca Schaeffer would become his girlfriend but that impossible dream was now crushed by harsh reality.

It later transpired that Robert John Bardo was highly disturbed and dangerous. He had once stalked the doomed child peace activist Samantha Smith and tried to get onto the set of My Sister Sam. Bardo was said to be angry at Rebecca Schaeffer because she'd done a love scene in the film Scenes from the Class Struggle in Beverly Hills. This went against the wholesome sitcom image he had of Schaeffer in his warped imagination. Basically, Robert John Bardo was completely crazy. Not only that but he had a gun on him as he sat in the diner eating cheesecake and simmering with anger at how Schaeffer had not been terribly pleased to see him on her doorstep earlier.

Bardo decided to go back to the Mock Tudor House and talk to Schaeffer again. This happened about an hour after he'd first spoken to her. When she answered the door again Rebecca Schaeffer was understandably annoyed and frustrated to see Bardo standing there again. Schaeffer told Bardo that she'd been patient and signed an autograph for him but he was now harassing her and wasting her day with these interruptions. She told Bardo to leave her alone. At this Bardo produced his gun (which he was carrying around in a plastic bag) and shot her in the stomach. Schaeffer sank to the floor holding her stomach in confusion. "Why?" she said to Bardo. Why had he shot her? There was no logical answer to that question. Robert John Bardo was simply a disturbed and dangerous young man. It was probably inevitable that he would do something tragic one day.

A lot of people in the street apparently heard the screams of Rebecca Schaeffer that day. Bardo ran away as fast as he could. Rebecca Schaeffer was taken to hospital but pronounced dead within an hour. Bardo fled back to his home in Tuscon after the murder but was swiftly arrested by the police. One of Bardo's sisters knew that her brother suffered from mental illness and was obsessed with Rebecca Schaeffer. When she heard that Schaeffer had been murdered she immediately suspected her brother and called the police. This was only a day after his fateful encounter with Rebecca Schaeffer.

Bardo confessed to the murder straight away when he was taken into custody. He was found guilty of first degree murder in 1991 and sentenced to life imprisonment without the possibility of parole. Bardo gave an eccentric performance at the trial. When they played the U2 song in court that Bardo had apparently been inspired by, Bardo started singing along and dancing in his seat. It was pretty clear that this man was seriously crazy. The most chilling thing about this awful case was the ease with which Bardo managed to find out where Schaeffer lived. Bardo had hired a private investigator and the investigator simply found Schaeffer's address through the California Department of Motor Vehicles. Bardo could have actually done this himself and saved some money but he was obviously too stupid to work it out.

The tragic death of Rebecca Schaeffer triggered new anti-stalking laws. As a result of Rebecca's murder, Congress passed the Driver's Privacy Protection Act (which prohibits state Departments of Motor Vehicles from revealing the home addresses of state residents). The damage had already been done though. Bardo gave an interview in prison in which he said that if he had one wish it would be that Rebecca Schaeffer was still alive. Well, it was a bit late for that wasn't it? Maybe you shouldn't have shot her in the first place. In 2007, Bardo suffered a nasty prison attack in which he was stabbed eleven times. He somehow survived though. At the time of writing, Bardo is still imprisoned at the Avenal State Prison in Avenal, Calif.

Rebecca Schaeffer's boyfriend at the time of her death was the writer and director Brad Silberling. He based his 2002 film Moonlight Mile on her murder. Rebecca was buried at the Ahavai Sholom Cemetery in Portland, Multnomah County, Oregon. The murder of Rebecca Schaeffer remains one of the most chilling examples of 'stalking' ever recorded in Hollywood. It was a horrible and dreadfully sad case. The only crumb of comfort was the fact the fact that Rebecca's death did tighten the law and make such things more difficult to happen in the future. Rebecca's father campaigned for tighter gun control laws in the wake of her death. Any society that enabled people like Robert John Bardo to easily purchase guns clearly needed to have a serious think about its laws.

DCI Hamish Campbell believed that Barry George was Fulham's version of Robert John Bardo and Jill Dando was his Rebecca Schaeffer. What the police had to do now though was prove that George had murdered Dando. It wasn't enough to say that Barry George was creepy or odd or disturbed. It wasn't enough to say he read gun magazines and had once had a go on a rifle range. It wasn't enough to say that he was a sex pest who creeped women out. The police would have to prove that Barry George had murdered Jill Dando. The police needed firm evidence to link him to the crime. To this end the police took a coat from Barry George's flat. Fifteen days later the coat was taken to the Forensic Science Service. This happened in May 2000. What the police did with the coat for the intervening two weeks was never explained. It later transpired that the coat was photographed by the police at a studio. This studio had also been used to photograph firearms. You can see an obvious problem here already can't you?

The police then came up with what they believed was (finally) their trump card. The piece of conclusive evidence they had been desperately groping for ever since the shambling figure of Barry George shuffled onto their radar. They found a speck of firearms residue on the coat belonging to Barry George which they claimed matched the weapon used on Jill Dando. Firearm residue refers to the small particles, usually in the form of burnt or unburnt gunpowder, lead, and other abrasive materials, that are left behind on surfaces after a firearm is discharged. These residues can be found on the hands, clothing, or any other object that may have come in contact with the firearm or its discharge.

Firearm residue is significant in forensic investigations as it can provide important evidence related to a shooting incident. When a firearm is discharged, the hot gases and debris are expelled from the barrel, leaving behind residue on the shooter's hands, clothing, and surrounding surfaces. By analysing this residue, forensic scientists can determine if a person has recently fired a gun. Various methods can be used to collect gunshot residue, such as swabbing the shooter's hands, clothing, or surfaces in the vicinity of the shooting. These samples are then examined under a microscope or analysed using chemical tests to identify the presence of characteristic particles, such as lead, barium, and antimony. However, it is important to note that the presence of firearm residue does not necessarily indicate guilt or involvement in a crime. Residue can also be transferred secondarily, for example, by coming into contact with someone or something that has recently been in close proximity to a discharged firearm.

Case closed thought (or at least HOPED) the Met police. Well, hold on a minute. Given that the coat was photographed in a studio where firearms had also been photographed didn't this make the evidence invalid due to possible contamination? Besides, half the population of London, if subjected to forensic scrutiny, might be found to have a miniscule speck of firearms residue on them simply from brushing against someone on public transport. This type of evidence had never been used to convict someone before and it hasn't been used to convict someone since. It was a precarious and risky piece of evidence to build an entire case on but the police didn't see it like this at all. They felt the coat had Barry George banged to rights. But did it? Was the forensic evidence really strong enough to convict a man of murder?

Forensic evidence refers to the tangible materials and data that are collected, analysed, and presented in a court of law to establish facts related to a crime or legal investigation. It plays a crucial role in criminal investigations as it provides objective and scientific information that aids in determining guilt or innocence.

While forensic evidence is highly valuable and often considered solid proof in criminal investigations, it is not infallible. Factors such as contamination, human error, or the limitations of scientific techniques can introduce potential inaccuracies. Therefore, it is crucial for all evidence to undergo rigorous scrutiny and for the legal system to consider additional factors, such as eyewitness testimonies and motive, in conjunction with forensic evidence to ensure a fair and just trial.

It was later established that police firearms officers had been with Barry George at one point in this investigation - meaning the firearms residue could actually have come from them. The police seemed to be going out of their way to pin the murder on Barry George - however vague the evidence might be (and the evidence in this case seemed very vague). It much later transpired that Barry George loved fireworks and used to keep them in his pocket. It could well have been a firework that created the alleged gunshot residue. The police case against Barry George was dubious at best. They made great play of the fact that firearms residue had been found on his clothing but this was later proven to be so miniscule that it proved nothing at all.

Another ongoing problem with the police investigation is

that they made out that Barry George was some sort of gun expert or gun collector. He was nothing of the sort. The guns in his flat were basically toys. Barry George was a man who lived in his own fantasy world and one of his biggest 'fantasy games' was to pretend he was in the SAS. Just because someone is interested in guns and the military it doesn't mean that they are experts in this field or actually go around shooting people. One of the gun magazines in George's flat had an article about reactivating a deactivated pistol but the tools neccessary for such a task were never found in any of Barry George's possessions. No live working firearms were found in Barry George's flat either. He did not own a real gun.

One piece of evidence which seemed to make it unlikely that Barry George killed Jill Dando was the fact she was killed at 11-30am. Staff at the Hammersmith and Fulham Action on Disability centre told the police that on this very morning Barry George visited their offices at 11-50am and seemed perfectly calm and normal. How could Barry George have murdered Jill Dando, fled the scene, crept back to his flat, had a wash, changed his clothes, and then got to the Hammersmith and Fulham Action on Disability centre all inside twenty minutes? Well, as we shall see later, some have disputed this apparent alibi and think it would have been perfectly possible to do this walk in that time frame. It is true that Barry George knew these streets well and would therefore have known the quickest route.

Some of the neighbours of Jill Dando reported that they saw a man walking away in the area shortly after the murder but when these neighbours viewed a police identification line-up that included Barry George they failed to point him out. In fact, only one eyewitness described a man who could be construed as looking like Barry George. Barry George's defence team at the trial were especially strong when it came to demolishing the eyewitness evidence of the prosecution (but as we know that was all to no avail). The evidence from eyewitnesses was certainly confusing. Two people said they saw a man in a coat near Gowan Avenue shortly after the murder while others said they saw a man in a suit jogging as if he was in a great hurry. A few people reported a Range Rover acting suspiciously (one woman said the Range Rover had been impatiently revved up behind her in traffic as if the driver was in a great rush). All of this may or may not have been relevant because people in suits in a rush and impatient drivers are not exactly unheard of in west London.

A man named Barry Lindsay later told the media that he had driven past Jill Dando's home on the morning of the murder and seen her struggling on her front path with a man - who was obviously the killer. Mr Lindsay said the man struggling with Jill Dando definitely wasn't Barry George but when he went to the police to report what he had seen they were not interested. "I told officers they needed to find a man with olive skin, dark hair and who looked like he was of Mediterranean origin. But straight off, they said, 'We are looking at a local guy over this murder. He is called Barry George'. They asked if I knew him and described what he looked like. But I told them, 'That's not the man I saw – I am 100 per cent sure of it'. As soon as those words left my mouth I felt like the police didn't want to listen any more. The way they acted really took me by surprise."

Barry Lindsay said he did not stop and go to assist Jill Dando - though he hit his brakes and thought about it. He presumed she was involved in some domestic dispute (Mr Lindsay obviously had no idea a murder was about to take place) with a boyfriend or something. Lindsay said that he had intervened in a public domestic dispute before and ended up in court as a consequence after having to fight the man involved. He was therefore in no hurry to repeat that experience. Mr Lindsay said that the police took him to the crime scene at Gowan Avenue but kept asking him if the person he saw could have been Barry George. When he repeatedly insisted that the man he had seen with Jill Dando looked nothing like Barry George the police lost interest in him and never contacted him again. Mr Lindsay was understandably perplexed and astonished by this given that he appeared to be the most important eyewitness in that he'd actually seen the man who who killed Jill Dando!

CHAPTER FIVE

The police psychological reports attributed all manner of things to Barry George. They suggested he had believed he had some sort of special relationship with Jill Dando because she read the news and so stared straight into the camera as she spoke. They suggested that Barry George had interpreted the colour of Jill Dando's clothes on television as coded messages to him. None of this was provable though. It was all complete nonsense. There was also a disconnect between the actual MO of the crime and the capabilities of the prime suspect. The killer had been highly efficient and also displayed no small degree of cunning in escaping from the scene. Efficiency and cunning were not words that readily came to mind when describing Barry George. Barry George was a clumsy and slow man who was easily confused and lazily ambled through life in a vacant world of his own.

George suffered from epilepsy - which made him slow and sluggish. Epilepsy is a neurological disorder that affects the brain and causes recurring seizures. These seizures are caused by abnormal brain activity, and often result in convulsions, loss of consciousness, or abnormal behaviours. There are many different types of epilepsy, and the severity and frequency of seizures can vary greatly from person to person. Some individuals may only experience occasional seizures, while others may have multiple seizures in a day.

Epilepsy can be caused by a variety of factors, including genetics, brain injuries, infections, and developmental disorders. In some cases, the cause of epilepsy may be unknown.

Barry George also had a low IQ which made even the simplest task difficult for him. "He's the sort of bloke, you throw him a tennis ball and he'll miss it," one of Barry George's friends later told a documentary. George hadn't done himself too many favours with his evidence - although this was presumably because he wasn't very bright rather than sinister misdirection. When he was first spoken to by detectives, Barry George told the police he had no idea who Jill Dando was - which was plainly ludicrous. Of course he knew who she was. She lived in the next street. Barry George saying in 1999 he had no idea who Jill Dando was would be like someone in the Britain of 2023 saying they'd never heard of Phillip Schofield. You'd have to be living in a cave with no access to television or newspapers not to know who Jill Dando was in 1999. Jill Dando was all over the news because she'd just been murdered! George told a reporter that he used to watch Crimewatch so he patently knew who Jill Dando was.

Barry George also told the police he had never heard of Gowan Avenue. This was obviously dubious given that he used to visit a doctor there and it was a stone's throw from his flat. Still, Barry George did have an awful lot of different doctors and wasn't very good with names so it is just about possible (if unlikely) he had walked up this street numerous times without having the faintest idea what it was called. Barry George was seen putting some flowers at the spot where Dando was murdered so he definitely knew of Gowan Avenue. The fact that George lived so close to Dando was actually a weakness when it came to eyewitness evidence. The people in those immediate streets must have seen the unmistakable figure of Barry George ambling around many times in the previous months and years. You'd think that if it really was him who fled the scene after the murder that someone would have recognised him. If it had been him who killed Jill Dando why had not a single person identified Barry George as a person seen shuffling away after the murder?

Barry George was a very distinctive looking man with his protruding lower lip, hefty build, and narrow eyes. This is clearly a man you would recognise if you were shown a photo of him. The prosecution relied on some witnesses who said they had seen George in the area when the murder took place but these witnesses said they could not be certain. Several of the witnesses said the suspect had long hair. Barry George always had closely cropped hair. Another big factor in this case which the police seemed to curiously ignore is that the area of Fulham where Jill Dando was murdered was a pretty well-heeled sort of place and had an extensive CCTV camera system. And yet not a single one of these cameras picked up any footage of Barry George in the area on the morning of the murder either before, during, or after the crime.

You can only convict someone of a murder if you can place them at the scene of the crime at the time of the murder. The police could not do this so put all their chips on the firearms reside - which, as we have noted, seemed a rather dubious and unconvincing piece of evidence upon which to convict a man of murder. The other evidence against Barry George was purely circumstantial. Although he was clearly a dodgy character with some sexual type offences on his slate there was still no evidence at all that he had an 'obsession' with Jill Dando. Barry George was actually charged with Jill Dando's murder only three days after his arrest on 25 May 2000. The police believed George was lying about having no interest in Jill Dando. They were certain that he was the killer.

George's barrister at the first trial was the famous Michael Mansfield. Michael Mansfield is known for his work in defending high-profile and controversial cases, including those involving political activists and victims of miscarriages of justice. Mansfield has represented clients such as the Birmingham Six, the Blackburn Three, and the family of Stephen Lawrence, a black teenager who was murdered in a racially motivated attack in London in 1993. Mansfield was called to the Bar in 1967 and began practicing as a barrister in 1969. He has been involved in a wide range of legal areas, including civil liberties, public inquiries, and criminal law. Mansfield has also been involved in international cases, including the Lockerbie trial, the Bloody Sunday inquiry, and the inquest into the death of Princess Diana. Throughout his career, Mansfield has been a vocal advocate for human rights and has been involved in efforts to reform the legal system. At one point Mansfield tried tro get the Jill Dando trial aborted on the grounds that Barry George was getting so much bad press in the media that a fair trial was impossible.

Although some months passed before the police spoke to him about Jill Dando's murder, Barry George had been on the police radar for a long time due to complaints made against him by women. George was also briefly (and ludicrously you might venture) a suspect in the murder of Rachel Nickell on Wimbledon Common in 1992. Rachel was with her two-year old son at the time and stabbed nearly fifty times. Her throat was slit and she was sexually assaulted. It was a horrendous attack. A man named Colin Stagg was later arrested for the murder but he was completely innocent of this crime and received substantial police compensation. In 2004, new forensic techniques connected Robert Napper to the murder of Rachel Nickell. He was convicted on manslaughter charges for this murder in 2008 because of diminished responsibility.

A woman named Susan Mayes, who lived on Gowan Avenue, was the only eyewitness who identified Barry George as a man she had seen acting suspiciously in the street on the morning of the murder. This sighting took place at seven in the morning as Mayes was leaving her house to go to work. However it was a full year after the murder before Mayes identified Barry George to the police - by which time his appearance had changed in that he had put on weight and grown a beard. At the trial Michael Mansfield was able to get Mayes to admit she had only seen the 'suspicious man' for five or six seconds at best before she departed. The man had apparently turned away and started wiping a car window. It was certainly far from conclusive that this man was really Barry George.

There was another problem with the eyewitness evidence of Susan Mayes. Barry George didn't have a car and didn't drive. Another person reported seeing a man in that location around seven in the morning but they said there was no car. It seems most likely that this was just an innocent member of the public. Mayes actually also told the police that the man was of Mediterranean appearance. This is exactly what

Barry Lindsay, the eyewitness the police - for reasons best known to themselves - chose to ignore said to the police too. Michael Mansfield was able to pour a lot of cold water on the eyewitness evidence of the police and prosecution.

The trial spent three days on the gunshot particle evidence presented by the police. The prosecution said the particle matched the chemical residue left on Jill Dando's hair and coat. They believed that Barry George had shot Jill Dando and then put the gun in his pocket and this is why there was foresic evidence in his coat. The prosecution said the chances of contamination were remote. The defence had a gunshot expert named John Loyd in court. Lloyd said that a single gunshot particle was such a flimsy piece of evidence that it was hardly worth talking about. This speck could have come from anywhere. There is evidence that some of the police officers who searched Barry George's flat were armed. The firearms particle could actually have come from one of them. This was all obviously the strategy of the defence. They argued that contamination was the most logical explanation for the particle. The police insisted though that their protocols and handling of the forensic evidence had been professional and proper.

The prosecution painted Barry George as a gun nut with some expertise in these matters. They said two blank guns were found in his flat and seemed to suggest he owned a real gun which he had managed to hide. There was a problem though with this evidence which connected to the particle of gunshot residue. Barry George's flat was a dump. It was strewn with rubbish and newspapers and hadn't seen a hoover or polish cloth in years. And yet only one particle of gunshot residue was found. If he had a live gun or had really shot Jill Dando wouldn't they have found more forensic evidence in his flat given that he never cleaned it?

The prosecution clearly struggled when it came to the motive for the murder. They pointed out that George had several newspapers and magazines with Jill Dando memorials in his flat. So what? Barry George never threw anything away and magazines and newspapers were full of Jill Dando memorials and stories in the aftermath of her murder. Michael Mansfield pointed out that none of these Dando memorials had been cut out or given any special resting place. In fact there wasn't any evidence that Barry George had even read them. The prosecution suggested that Barry George had a grudge against the BBC because of the way they had treated his hero Freddie Mercury. This was thin evidence indeed and hardly worthy of a murder trial.

One area in the trial where the prosecution did have some success was with Barry George's visit to the Hammersmith and Fulham Action on Disability centre on the morning of Jill Dando's murder. Barry George said he had arrived there at 11-50 and this was initially confirmed by staff. That basically gave Barry George an alibi because it was hard to see how he could have murdered Dando, fled the scene, disposed of the gun, changed his clothes, and then walked to the centre in that time frame. However the prosecution managed to obtain statements from other staff at the centre who say Barry George arrived later than 11-50 am. This evidence therefore contradicted an alibi. There was also evidence that Barry George had gone back to the centre and also a taxi company a few days after Dando's murder to ask if they could help confirm his movements on the morning of Dando's killing. As we have noted, Barry George said he did this merely because he knew the police would talk to him but it was suspicious all the same. The usually unflappable Michael Mansfield suddenly found himself batting on a sticky wicket during this part of the trial.

Judge William Gage told the jury that they could convict Barry George if they felt it had been proven that he was in Gowan Avenue at the time of the murder and had also gone back to the Hammersmith and Fulham Action on Disability centre in search of an alibi. The latter was already proven while the former was never established. Here's the most incredible thing about the first trial though. Gage told the jury that the gunshot particle evidence was not important. They did not have to find this evidence conclusive in order to convict Barry George. They simply had to decide on whether it was proven that George was on Gowan Avenue and that he had sought an alibi. As you might imagine, Barry George's defence team were annoyed and flabbergasted by this because they felt the gunshot particle was a very weak piece of evidence.

In 2001, despite the apparently flimsy nature of the case against him, Barry George was sentenced to life in prison for Jill Dando's murder. The jury found him guilty by a 10-1 verdict. It was a conviction which troubled many because the evidence seemed far from conclusive. There was a degree of surprise at the verdict because many observers felt there wasn't sufficient evidence to convict Barry George. It was never even proven that he was at the scene of the murder on the morning in question.

George showed no emotion at the verdict and calmly shuffled out of the court. He gave no indication that he even knew what was happening to him. He had been unable to defend himself or be cross examined because he wasn't mentally capable of this. One of his defence team described Barry George's brain as being like 'flickering light bulb'. At the end of the trial, during the summing up, George's barrister Michael Mansfield told the court that Serbians were probably responsible for the murder. Mansfield said that Eastern European ammunition was used. The jury obviously didn't buy this explanation though.

The gunshot particle which had helped convict Barry George had been presented at the trial by Robin Keeley of the Forensic Science Service. Here's the thing though. After the trial Keely began to have severe misgivings about this crucial piece of evidence. He considered it a 'neutral' piece of evidence. Other forensic scientists shared this view. They believed it was ridiculous that a man had been convicted of murder partly because of a microscopic particle which in all likelihood was a result of contamination. It took some time for this information to be revealed though - during which time the bewildered Barry George languished in prison.

The police still believed Barry George was the killer and the newspapers endlessly ran lurid stories about this 'Jill Dando obsessed nutter' who had shot the newsreader. It turned out though that this sorry affair was a miscarriage of justice. It later transpired that the police found 800 newspapers in George's flat and only eight contained pieces about Jill Dando. That was hardly an obsession was it? The conviction of Barry George seemed precarious and unconvincing at best so it was no surprise that it ultimately fell apart under fresh and persistent legal scrutiny from Barry George's lawyers in the years to come.

After three appeals, the conviction of Barry George was quashed in 2008 and he was finally set free. Once the gun particle evidence was debunked the police and prosecution had absolutely nothing else up their sleeve to pin the murder on Barry George. More than anything it was the indefatigable campaigning of Barry George's sister Michelle Bates that got him out of prison. Michelle believed that her brother's epilepsy would have made it impossible for him to successfully carry out this murder. George was denied compensation by the Ministry of Justice and refused compensation at the Court of Appeal in 2013 for his wrongful conviction as he was deemed "not innocent enough".

The basic difference between the two trials was that in the second trial the particle evidence was not permitted because it was deemed unsafe and controversial. The prosecution were though allowed to tell the jury in the second trial about Barry George's history of harassing women (this evidence had, for some reason, not been permitted in the first trial). Without the particle evidence the prosecution plainly struggled. All the new stuff about Barry George harassing women and following them, as grim and sordid as it was, didn't really seem to help them much either. It could be the case that the jury found this evidence was not relevant to the question of whether or not George killed Jill Dando. The prosecution needed to prove that Barry George was a ruthless killer. That he had shot someone. The fact that he had pestered women on the street was a grim commentary on his character but it wasn't proof that he was a murderer.

Barry George said that after his release from prison he was constantly followed and threatened by the police. His family feared that the police were going to stitch Barry George up on some other charges as revenge for his successful appeal so they took the wise and logical precaution of getting him out of the country. Barry George went to live in Ireland where his sister lived. It is somewhat ironic that Barry George, a man who always yearned for fame and attention, did actually become famous in the end and even appeared on television after he was released from prison. This was though not a fame you would really wish on anyone. Despite what had happened to him it was impossible for Barry

George to be a sympathetic figure because his grim history of harassing women had now come to light. The fear of scrutiny over this was probably a factor in why Barry George's sister decided to drag her brother out of the limelight and insist that he lead a quiet and private life in Ireland.

Despite the overturning of the conviction, Hamish Balfour remained convinced that Barry George was the killer of Jill Dando. He's not alone. Dando's former Crimewatch co-host Nick Ross has suggested on his website that he is far from convinced that Barry George was really innocent. Having laid out many reasons why George was innocent let's flip this upside down and see if we can construct a plausible case for why Barry George might have been the killer. Is it at all possible he really did kill Jill Dando but managed to fool everyone? Those inclined to have sympathy for this theory would argue that Hamish Balfour did not set out to 'stitch' Barry George up for the crime but in fact went out of his way to eliminate George from the investigation. It was only when George's evidence proved a mass of lies and contradictions and his alarming history of stalking women came to light that Barry George became a suspect.

The police could point out too that it wasn't them who went out looking for Barry George or a Barry George type character. He only became a suspect because of persistent phone calls to the police from people who knew George. These people told the police to check out Barry George because they thought he was a wrong 'un who displayed very creepy behaviour around women. We can place Barry George in Fulham at the time of the murder (which is obviously a good start) because he lived there. He knew the area well. It doesn't seem unreasonable to think that George knew Dando had a house in the area. He might even have seen her walking around or driving down the street. What we can't do though is place George on Gowan Avenue at the time of the murder. It is possible he was there but no eyewitness evidence or CCTV proved this without a shadow of doubt (and if you are going to convict a man of murder you really need no doubt at all).

One could argue that Barry George was not as inert and inept as was made out. He was clever enough to have duped people into thinking he was a karate champion and owned companies so he couldn't have been that stupid. And a man capable of sneaking into the grounds of the royal family would clearly be capable of following a celebrity on the street and deducing where she lived. Admittedly though the Barry George of 1999 had deteriorated both mentally and physically. You can see already can't you that it is not easy to write about Barry George being guilty? There are too many weaknesses in the case against him. Let's press on anyway and continue to try.

Some of those who know something about crime and guns are not wholly convinced by the theory that Jill Dando was killed by a professional hitman. They point out that the street where she was killed was a terrible place to murder someone because it was a long street with no quick exits. It would have made much more sense for a hitman to kill Jill Dando at her home in Chiswick. It could also be pointed out that there was never any proof of a 'getaway' driver - which is definitely something a professional hitman might have employed.

Barry George had visited the Hammersmith and Fulham Action Centre on the morning of Dando's murder to discuss his accommodation. He later returned and asked them what time he had been there on the day on Dando's murder. He did the same with a taxi company. This sounds a lot like someone seeking an alibi (the prosecution, as we have noted, used this detail to their advantage in the first trial and definitely got Michael Mansfield playing off the back foot). It also explains how George - if he was the killer - got to the centre so quickly. He could maybe have used a taxi. Besides, some would contend that George could easily have walked it inside twenty minutes if he was brisk.

When George was later asked by the police why he had visited the centre and taxi company again, he replied that he did so because he knew with his history that the police would question him over Dando's murder sooner or later so he wanted to account for his movements. That could be construed as a good answer or as some mild admission of guilt depending on which way you care to look at it. The gun used in the murder was something akin to a modified starter pistol (it is obviously impossible to turn a starter pistol into a weapon but you know what I mean). Would any professional criminal really have used such a weapon with the risk of it jamming? Also, Jill Dando had her key in the front door when she was shot. She was about to go inside. Why did the killer not push her inside the door and shoot her there in private rather than on the front path? A professional might have done that.

Police experts believed Dando was killed by someone with a personality disorder - and this certainly applied to Barry George. Personality disorder refers to a mental health condition characterised by patterns of unhealthy and inflexible thinking, behaviour, and functioning. This disorder typically affects the way individuals perceive and relate to others and themselves, leading to difficulties in social interactions, work, and personal relationships. There are various types of personality disorders, including borderline, antisocial, narcissistic, avoidant, dependent, and others. Each type has its own set of symptoms and can significantly impact a person's daily life and well-being.

As for the particle of gunshot residue, well, that was always the nub of the case. It was an unsafe way to convict someone of murder but all the same it is theoretically possible that this particle was genuine and came from the murder of Jill Dando. As you can see then, one can paint a picture where Barry George is less innocent than he might appear from the standard line that he was some dimwitted patsy the police zeroed in on in a grave miscarriage of justice. That said though it is a lot more difficult to write about WHY Barry George killed Jill Dando than it is to write about why he DIDN'T kill Jill Dando.

When you weigh up the evidence available it is simply not conclusive enough to say with any certainty at all that Barry George was responsible for Jill Dando's murder. One suspects that you could have taken any number of 'oddball loners' in the west London of 1999 and constructed a case of circumstantial evidence which suggested they killed Jill Dando. That is not enough though. You need hard hard forensic evidence or CCTV. You need eyewitnesses who dovetail. You need more of a case than the fact that Barry George lived in Fulham and had a couple of newspapers with a photo of Jill Dando.

A salient problem with the case against Barry George is that the police and prosecution never came up with a motive. Given that Barry George displayed no particular interest in Jill Dando at all why on earth would he suddenly decide to kill her? Barry George had also pestered dozens of women but he'd never killed any of them or even attempted to. He was clearly a deeply weird person who could be unpleasant but there was never any evidence that he was capable of murder. The case against Barry George - ultimately - was not convincing. It seems highly unlikely that he was the killer. Not impossible but unlikely.

CHAPTER SIX

This now begs an obvious question. If Barry George was innocent then who really killed Jill Dando? There were a number of other theories. Because she had hosted Crimewatch (a show which is obviously all about catching criminals and solving crimes) there was an obvious theory that an embittered criminal might have killed Dando in revenge. Maybe the show had put someone behind bars or mentioned some criminal or other and this criminal or their associates (or indeed even relatives) had taken revenge by shooting Dando?

While this 'embittered criminal' theory was one that seemed reasonable to investigate it did not seem to yield any great leads or lines of inquiry for the Met. The police said they investigated every single Crimewatch appeal that Jill Dando had hosted but nothing came of this.

However, just because the Met could find no evidence of a criminal conspiracy it doesn't mean that one didn't exist. The use of police informants is a controversial practice, as it raises ethical concerns and potential risks. There is always a risk that informants may be unreliable, have ulterior motives, or provide false information. Furthermore, the reliance on informants can sometimes compromise the integrity of investigations, as they may be involved in criminal activities themselves and continue to engage in such activities while working as informants. There were certainly rumours that in the criminal underworld informers were warned to keep quiet about the Jill Dando murder.

There are stories that an intelligence report suggested one of London's most notorious crime families might have killed Dando but the Met Police declined to investigate this lead because their blinkers were too firmly fixed on the shambling figure of Barry George. Whether it was through the disinterest of the police or lack of evidence (maybe it was a combination of both?), the end result was that - officially at least - no criminal was ever seriously or credibly connected to Dando's murder through anything that had appeared on Crimewatch. This theory certainly has more plausibility than many others though. Though some dismiss this theory out of hand the fact that Dando was a presenter for a show that had the specific aim of catching criminals can't be ignored.

Mark Williams-Thomas, a former police officer turned crime investigator, believes that Jill Dando was killed by a professional hitman and says he has the name of the killer. Williams-Thomas doesn't think the murder of Jill Dando was an amateur job done by some deranged stalker. He showed an underworld hitman a list of police suspects in the Dando case and got an interesting response. "There are names here that I recognise, and there's one in particular that stands out to me," the hitman said. "But I wouldn't identify that person because it's very dangerous. I'm sure that they would come after me." Williams-Thomas believes it is 'pride' which prevents the police from admitting they messed up by charging Barry George with the murder. Williams-Thomas believes the Met should start the Jill Dando investigation afresh and focus on the criminal underworld.
Another theory was that the killer of Jill Dando was a

barman named Joe who lived in Spain. Joe was said to owe money to Kenneth Noye - a criminal who was put behind bars thanks partly to Crimewatch. Kenneth Noye gained notoriety for his involvement in various high-profile crimes. Born on May 24, 1948, in Bexleyheath, London, Noye was involved in smuggling stolen goods and organised crime during the 1980s and 1990s. One of Noye's most infamous crimes was the murder of a police officer in 1993. Noye became the prime suspect in the case due to his involvement in a road rage incident shortly before the murder. However, Noye was acquitted of the murder in 1996, much to the outrage of the public.

Prior to the murder case, Noye was known for his involvement in an infamous gold bullion heist in 1983. The heist resulted in the theft of approximately six tons of gold worth millions of pounds. Noye was eventually convicted for handling the stolen gold and was sentenced to 14 years in prison. In 1996, while serving his sentence, Noye was involved in a confrontation with another motorist, Stephen Cameron, on a motorway near Swanley, Kent. Noye stabbed Cameron to death during the altercation. He was later found guilty of murder in 2000 and sentenced to life imprisonment with a minimum tariff of 16 years.

Kenneth Noye's criminal activities and his ability to evade conviction in some cases have made him a notorious figure in the criminal underworld. He has been described as a skilled and ruthless criminal who operated within a network of organised crime. Despite being imprisoned, Noye's influence and reputation continue to intrigue and captivate the public's imagination. Alan Decabral, an eyewitness in the murder of Stephen Cameron, was later shot dead in what was clearly a professional hit. Curiously, Noye's barrister was Michael Mansfield. Mansfield went out of his way to discredit Decabral as a witness after Decabral had been shot dead! Suffice to say then, Noye had the connections to silence people. If he wanted someone dead he could arrange for that to happen.

Joe was said to live among gangster and criminal ex-pats in Spain and in order to clear his many debts agreed to go to London and stage a revenge killing on Dando. This theory was apparently floated by the National Criminal Intelligence Service. Whether it has any credibility or not though is open to question. The identity of 'Joe' was never established or verified. No one knows if he even existed in the first place. This theory is clearly not impossible but remains too vague to have ever gained much traction among the many competing theories concerning Jill Dando's murder. There is simply not enough evidence to take this theory seriously - interesting though it kight be.

As for the strange nature of the rather homemade weapon used in the Jill Dando killing, the police believed this was proof that the killer was an amateur. However the selection of this weapon was very shrewd because it could not be traced. The weapon also evidently did what it was designed to do in that - tragically - Jill Dando died as a consequence. None of these details suggest an amateur who had no idea what he was doing. Weapons expert Freddy Mead testified at the trial. Of the murder and weapon used he said - "It's hard to imagine how it could have been improved upon." Mead certainly didn't think the murder was done by a bungling amateur like Barry George.

One strange detail is that the killer closed the gate behind them as they went up the path to shoot Jill Dando. This led to an unlikely if interesting theory that the killer did this by instinct because they had been in that house before. This would obviously mean that Jill Dando was shot by someone she actually knew. This is regarded to be highly unlikely though and isn't at all taken seriously as a theory. This theory would mean Dando was killed by a relative, neighbour, or boyfriend and that was definitely ruled out.

The police had obviously scoured through Dando's past and private life to see if a scorned lover might potentially be responsible and have had a grudge against her but this failed to provide any notable leads or lines of enquiry.

There was no one in Dando's past or private life with any reason or motive to kill her. The police said they investigated about 2,000 suspects in this case - which would obviously have been a very laborious and lengthy task. At one point a cleaner who worked two doors up from Dando was questioned over the murder. The Met would argue that they left no stone unturned when they investigated this crime. Despite all the theories the police seemed resolute in their belief that this was a 'lone stalker' type of murder. This is the main reason why they became so obsessed with Barry George. The police built up a picture of the type of person who they thought probably killed Jill Dando and Barry George (unfortunately for him) ticked most of the boxes in that profile.

There is of course the possibility that Jill Dando was killed by another stalker who was in the Barry George mould. It was not proven that Barry George was the killer but given the strange ramshackle nature of the weapon used it seems possible that it could have been another 'amateur' killer from west London. What if there was someone who had become obsessed with Jill Dando and was angered when he learned that she was going to get married? Shortly before her death, Jill Dando had appeared on the cover of the Radio

Times dressed in leather. The article had noted that she was happily engaged and about to marry. Could this article have been the final 'trigger' for some nutty stalker?

It is plausible that a lone Jill Dando obsessed stalker existed who was not on the radar of the police. This person though would have to have no criminal record to have remained so elusive. Many believe the 'lone amateur' theory is more convincing than the theories that gangsters or foreign agents had Dando killed. A problem with this theory is that it seems unlikely that someone with stalker tendencies would not be known to the police. Stalkers tend not to suddenly come out of the blue. They usually establish a pattern of this behaviour and this what gets them caught. Here's another problem though with the lone stalker theory. There is no clear consensus on whether this killing had the hallmarks of a professional job.

The police felt the weapon and choice of location was against this 'professional' hitman theory. However, the murder was certainly efficient and the killer was elusive in the immediate aftermath of the crime. The killer shot Dando behind the ear so he knew where to shoot someone to ensure a quick death. This last detail is not indicative of someone who was a bungling amateur who had never done anything like this before. And how did the gunman managed to get away from the scene so successfully? This indicated some degree of research and planning (though by the same token it could be that the killer had some local knowledge of those streets). Those who lean towards the Serb/foreign agent theory think the killer probably got a flight straight out of London. Though the eyewitness evidence was not consistent and so never really proved anything one way or the other, many believe the killer used public transport to get out of Fulham.

Recently, court papers in France have suggested another theory in the murder of Jill Dando. The theory revolves around Gerald Marie. Gerald Marie is a former modelling agent and the ex-husband of supermodel Linda Evangelista. He was a prominent figure in the modelling industry, working for the prestigious Elite Model Management agency for many years. Marie was known for his influential role in discovering and representing top models, including Naomi Campbell, Gisele Bundchen, and Claudia Schiffer. However, his professional reputation was tarnished when he faced allegations of sexual misconduct and abuse by multiple models. In 2020, Marie was charged with rape and is currently awaiting trial. These allegations have brought attention to issues of exploitation and abuse in the modelling industry.

An investigative reporter named Lisa Brinkworth was involved in an undercover expose of Gerald Marie and accused him of sexual abuse. It is alleged in the court papers that the murder of Jill Dando might have been a case of mistaken identity. This theory basically goes like this. Gerald Marie wanted to silence Lisa Brinkworth so hired Russian gangsters to kill her. Brinklworth lived in Fulham and looked a bit like Jill Dando in that they were similar ages and both blonde. Anyway, the theory contends that the Russian hitman got his wires crossed and instead of shooting Brinkworth he shot Jill Dando. Brinkworth told the media - 'Even if there was a tiny possibility, I don't know if I could live with that, so I'm hoping there's nothing in that. I try not to think about it. I really, really don't want it to be true.'

Gerald Marie and his legal team vehemently deny the allegation that he arranged for Brinkworth to be shot and the hitman murdered Dando by mistake. Is this theory plausible? Well, it doesn't chime with the amateurish weapon used - though that could have been misdirection designed to make the police think a professional killer wasn't involved. The biggest problem with this theory though is the notion that a hired hitman would shoot the wrong person by mistake. This is something which has happened before but why would they get Jill Dando of all people - one of the most famous people in Britain - mixed up with Lisa Brinkworth? That doesn't really make any sense although the fact that they both worked for the BBC might possibly explain the confusion.

Omar Harfouch, an executive for Elite, says that in 1999 he was in the room when Marie asked the Russian Mafia to sort out the Brinkworth problem. Despite the headlines it earned, the Lisa Brinkworth theory in relation to the Jill Dando case is not one that many people find plausible at all. This theory is certainly entertaining and would make a good thriller story but it doesn't seem to have much basis in fact. If nothing else though it was another reminder that the murder of Jill Dando continues to leave a wave of theory and speculation in its wake. The challenge comes from sifting through these theories and deciding which one makes the most sense and is therefore the most likely explanation for why a television was shot on her doorstep one morning in 1999.

A former IRA member named Wayne Aird claimed that Dando had been killed by an IRA hit squad. While the IRA would doubtless have been capable of such an act this claim was never verified or proven. Aird said that he was part of a four man IRA hit squad that killed Dando in revenge for her activities on Crimewatch. He was serving time in Wakefield Prison for murder when he made these claims. According to Aird the IRA men escaped in Range Rovers and then hid in a London safehouse until the coast was clear. The police clearly did not take Aird very seriously because they declined to investigate his claim. One factor against this theory is the Northern Ireland peace process. At this delicate and historic time in Northern Ireland would the IRA and its political wing really have sanctioned the brazen assassination of a famous BBC presenter? It seems somewhat unlikely.

Aird though was apparently involved with the Real IRA - a dissident Irish republican paramilitary group who the 'official' Republican movement had far less sway over. The Real Irish Republican Army (Real IRA) is a dissident Irish republican paramilitary group that emerged in 1997. It originated from a split within the Provisional Irish Republican Army (IRA) during the Northern Ireland peace process. The Real IRA opposes the peace process and the Good Friday Agreement, which was a major step towards resolving the conflict in Northern Ireland. It advocates for a united Ireland achieved through armed struggle and has carried out several attacks targeting both security forces and civilians.

The group has been responsible for numerous bombings, shootings, and other violent acts since its formation. The 1998 Omagh bombing, which killed 29 people and injured around 220 others, is one of the most deadly attacks attributed to the Real IRA. This bombing greatly undermined support for the group and drew widespread condemnation. Over the years, the Real IRA has faced a significant crackdown by security forces on both sides of the Irish border. Many of its members have been arrested and convicted, leading to a decrease in its operational capacity. However, it remains a persistent threat, albeit diminished, and continues to engage in sporadic violence to further its cause. The group's activities have been widely condemned by the international community, political parties in Ireland, and the majority of the Irish population. Efforts to counter the Real IRA's activities involve cooperation between the police forces in Ireland and the United Kingdom, intelligence gathering, and increased security measures in areas at risk.

The Real IRA certainly never claimed the 'credit' for murdering Jill Dando - which was out of character for them. Why stage an audacious operation like this and let someone else take the credit? Leeds solicitor Stuart Page, who met and talked to Aird, wrote at the time: 'It is quite possible the contents of his statement are pure make-believe. However, that is not a view that I formed during my short meeting with Mr Aird.' In 1999. members of the Real IRA went to Croatia to purchase firearms in anticipation of a new terrorist campaign. It is even alleged that members of the Real IRA might have been paid by the Serbians to murder Jill Dando. This is a conflation of two theories to make a new super theory.

Though the IRA angle is interesting it seems less likely than British criminals murdering Dando. Aird wrote a letter to Barry George's legal team with these IRA allegations. The police were apparently shown the letter in 2008 but decided it wasn't worth investigating. Aird claimed that Dando was a target because of her links to the police through Crimewatch and that the Real IRA did not admit to the murder because they didn't want to wreck the peace process - which is odd because the Real IRA didn't actually agree with the peace process and Good Friday Agreement. As ever then with the Jill Dando case, the theories remain slightly clouded, very knotty, and difficult to judge.

CHAPTER SEVEN

In 2014 a former police officer, who didn't wish to be named, claimed in the media that the gun used to kill Jill Dando was later used in a gangland shooting in Liverpool. The police officer also claimed that they had secretly recorded criminals in Liverpool talking about Dando's murder and one of them said the contract to kill her came from a gangster in Scotland. This Scottish gangster was presumably moved to take action by something on Crimewatch. Other police officers dismissed the claims by this unnamed source though and said they were nonsense. If nothing else though this story was proof that the Crimewatch/criminal underworld theories in relation to Jill Dando's murder had never gone away. In fact, they were so persistent that this made them hard to ignore. Was it really unbelievable to think that Jill Dando had more chance of being murdered by a professional criminal or gangster than a random nutty stalker? This wasn't unbelievable at all. In fact it actually had some logic to it as a theory. There were a lot more underworld criminals in Britain in 1999 than there were Jill Dando obsessed stalkers with guns. In fact, I'd wager there were few if any of the latter.

The most outlandish theory in relation to this case is that Jill Dando was killed because she was about to expose a BBC paedophile ring. The general gist of this theory (which has inspired some crackpot David Icke style YouTube videos) is that Dando had encountered Jimmy Savile at the BBC and realised he was a sleaze and old lech. Jimmy Savile (1926-2011) was a television and radio personality who was well-known for his hosting roles on various radio and television shows, as well as his charity work. He got a knighthood and was friends with Margaret Thatcher and Prince Charles. However, after his death, numerous allegations of sexual abuse and misconduct came to light. Savile is now widely regarded as one of the UK's most prolific sexual offenders, with hundreds of victims coming forward. His actions have had a significant impact on the British media industry and have led to changes in how institutions handle allegations of abuse.

The theory is that Jill Dando had then learned of a sinister and all powerful celebrity and establishment paedophile ring in Britain which she decided to expose. This establishment paedophile ring decided they had to silence this pesky journalist and so arranged to have her killed on her doorstep. No doubt those who have peddled with conspiracy have powerful figures in the Met at the time as part of the conspiracy. Out of all the theories which have abounded since Jill Dando was shot this is by far the most fanciful explanation for her death. It seems rather far-fetched to think that Dando was killed by celebrity sex offenders or some establishment hit squad and, besides, the stories of an elite 'above the law' paedophile ring made up of celebrities and politicians were largely exposed as fiction thanks to the infamous Carl Beech affair.

Carl Beech was the man who claimed he and others had been abused at children's homes by a secret group of army officers, celebrities, and politicians who were perfectly willing to kill to cover up their tracks. Beech turned out to be a fantasist who was making it all up. Not only that but he had indecent images of children on his own computer. No doubt there (sadly) ARE child sex offenders among the elite and famous but not to the organised extent that Beech and his supporters falsely claimed. The problem with this conspiracy theory is that you end up down a bonkers rabbit hole where Ted Heath was a shapeshifting lizard who threw children off his yacht and every tragedy is a false flag operation orchestrated by the Illuminati. By following this conspiracy theory you end up in the company of people with some very unverified claims and often some very unpleasant views.

The Elm Guest House was a hotel in Rocks Lane, near Barnes Common in southwest London. This was allegedly supposed to be the hub for this sinister paedophile ring. Unfortunately though the 'expose' of Elm was by a former councillor and social worker named Chris Fay who turned out to be a fraud and hoaxer. Fay was jailed for defrauding pensioners. Carl Beech took up the conspiracy baton later on. The former Labour Deputy leader Tom Watson was among those duped by Beech but when the police investigated the claims there was no truth in them. Public figures like Edward Heath, Leon Brittan, Edwin Bramall, Harvey Proctor and others had their names dragged through due to these false allegations.

What fanned the flames of this conspiracy is that the Elm Guest House co-owner Carole Kasir was found guilty at the Old Bailey in 1983 of running a disorderly house and possessing obscene videos. Kasir said that her only crime had been to make the hotel 'gay friendly'. Soon though a conspiracy theory swirled up which had the hotel as a place where politicians and celebrities would meet to abuse and murder children! It was all nonsense of course but the conspiracy theorists got more ammunition in 1990 when Kasir died of an overdose. In the world of conspiracy theories a random tragedy is not possible. All random tragedies in the world of conspiracy theorists are false flag operations or establishment assassinations. The problem with these sort of conspiracy theories is they tend to stem from dangerous and ill-informed places where the truth is less important than the agenda.

Take the recent QAnon movement in the United States. QAnon is a far-right conspiracy theory that originated on an internet forum in 2017. It claims that a secret group of elite pedophiles is running a global child sex trafficking ring, and that Donald Trump is working behind the scenes to expose and dismantle this network. Supporters of QAnon believe in the existence of a high-ranking government insider known as "Q," who supposedly provides cryptic messages and predictions on online forums. QAnon has been debunked by numerous fact-checkers and has gained attention for promoting baseless claims, inciting real-world violence, and spreading misinformation.

These are the lunatics who got involved with a preposterous and patently untrue conspiracy theory which stated that the Democratic Party and celebrities used a pizzeria as the base for a child sex trafficking ring! "Pizzagate" is a conspiracy theory that emerged during the 2016 United States presidential election. It suggests that high-ranking Democratic Party officials and prominent individuals were involved in a child sex trafficking ring operating out of a pizza restaurant in Washington, D.C. The theory is based on misinterpretations of emails leaked from the Democratic National Committee (DNC) and Hillary Clinton's campaign chairman, John Podesta.

The conspiracy theory gained traction on social media platforms and in some online forums, leading to a public frenzy and significant repercussions. In December 2016, a man walked into the pizza restaurant mentioned in the conspiracy theory, wielding a rifle, and fired multiple shots, though no one was injured. This incident highlighted the real-world consequences that conspiracy theories can have when taken to extreme levels. However, the theory has been widely debunked by various credible sources, including law enforcement agencies and independent investigations. The FBI and Washington, D.C. Metropolitan Police Department found no evidence of any such trafficking ring or the involvement of high-ranking officials in illegal activities.

Conspiracy theories are theories or explanations that suggest that certain events or situations are the result of secretive, often malevolent, plots by powerful entities or groups. These theories typically lack substantial evidence and are often based on limited or distorted information. People may believe in conspiracy theories due to cognitive biases such as motivated reasoning, which leads them to accept evidence supporting their pre-existing beliefs while rejecting contrary evidence. This bias can hinder critical thinking and objective evaluation.

The craziest Jill Dando theory is that Jimmy Savile himself arranged for her to be killed! Clearly, Saville was an influential and cunning man with powerful friends. He hid his secret life well by posing as this eccentric and avuncular marathon running charity fundraiser. It is alleged that Saville had some links too to criminal figures. However, the notion that he took out a contract to have Jill Dando killed because she was onto him is utterly preposterous. If a secret paedophile ring made up of politicians and celebrities really did exist then such a group would surely wish to maintain a low profile. It's hard to see how murdering Jill Dando would be doing this!

A much more plausible theory concerning the murder is that Jill Dando was killed in connection with the situation in the former Yugoslavia. Dando had fronted a television aid appeal for Kosovar Albanian refugees. Kosovar Albanian refugees refer to Albanian people from Kosovo who have been forced to flee their homes due to conflict or persecution. The term emerged during the Kosovo War in the late 1990s when ethnic Albanians in Kosovo faced violence and discrimination under the Serbian government. Many Kosovo Albanians sought refuge in neighbouring countries such as Albania, Macedonia, Montenegro, and further afield in Western Europe and North America.

During the war, Serbian forces carried out a campaign of ethnic cleansing against the Kosovo Albanian population, resulting in massive displacement. It is estimated that around one million Kosovo Albanians were displaced during the conflict. Many sought refuge in camps or with host families in neighbouring countries, while others embarked on dangerous journeys to seek safety elsewhere. In response to the crisis, humanitarian organizations and host countries worked to provide assistance and support to the refugees.

Temporary camps were established to provide shelter, food, and medical assistance. The international community also intervened, with NATO launching a military intervention to stop the violence in Kosovo. In the years following the conflict, some of the refugees returned to Kosovo as conditions improved, while others chose to establish new lives in their host countries. Today, there is still a significant population of Kosovar Albanian refugees and their descendants living in various parts of the world. They continue to face challenges related to integration, citizenship, and preserving their cultural identity.

Only two days before Jill Dando was killed, NATO had bombed Radio Television of Serbia's (RTS) headquarters - killing numerous employees. On April 23, 1999, at around 2:06 AM local time, NATO warplanes struck the RTS building, which was the main broadcasting station of Serbia. The NATO planes which took part in the attack took off from RAF

Fairford in Gloucestershire. The attack resulted in significant damage to the building, including the collapse of several floors. Additionally, 16 RTS employees were killed, and several others were injured. NATO justified the airstrike by claiming that the RTS headquarters was used as a propaganda tool by the then-President of Serbia, Slobodan Milosevic, to fuel ethnic hatred during the conflict in Kosovo.

However, this attack was highly controversial and drew international criticism. It was argued that targeting a civilian broadcasting station violated the principles of international humanitarian law. Human Rights Watch stated that the attack was an unlawful act of revenge rather than a military objective. Furthermore, the International Criminal Tribunal for the former Yugoslavia (ICTY) later indicted the NATO leaders responsible for the RTS bombing for violations of the laws and customs of war. Nevertheless, the charges were eventually dropped, as the court concluded that they did not amount to a criminal act. The bombing of RTS headquarters remains a contentious event, with differing opinions on the legality and moral justification of the attack.

The general theory then is that Dando was killed in retaliation for the bombing of Radio Television of Serbia's (RTS) headquarters. RTS was like Serbia's version of the BBC - for whom Dando had obviously worked. It was an eye for an eye revenge killing (according to the theory). The 'hit' on Dando was what you might describe as professional in that she was killed quickly and efficiently and the perpetrator fled the scene in fairly swift and elusive fashion. This obviously suggested that the killer was a trained hired professional and not some lone nutcase (like Barry George for example). If you believe in the Serbian theory then you most likely take the view that the murder of Jill Dando was professional in its MO.

Arkan, the Serbian warlord, is often alleged to have been the person who ordered the hit on Jill Dando. He died though so it would impossible to question him about it now. Arkan, whose real name was Željko Ražnatović, was a Serbian warlord and politician. He was born on April 17, 1952, in Brežice, Yugoslavia (now Slovenia). Arkan gained prominence in the 1990s during the Yugoslav Wars, particularly in the Croatian War and the Bosnian War. Arkan formed and led a paramilitary group called the Serb Volunteer Guard, also known as the "Arkan's Tigers." This group was notorious for its involvement in numerous war crimes and atrocities against non-Serb civilians. They were responsible for acts of ethnic cleansing, mass killings, looting, and persecution, particularly in Croatia and Bosnia and Herzegovina.

Arkan's Tigers became well-known for their brutal tactics, including forced deportations, sexual assault, and torture. Arkan himself was implicated in multiple war crimes, including the shelling of civilians and executions. Despite his criminal activities, Arkan pursued a political career and was elected as a member of the Serbian Radical Party. He also founded the Party of Serbian Unity. However, his political career was short-lived as he was assassinated in Belgrade on January 15, 2000, by a group of unknown assailants. Arkan's legacy remains controversial, with some seeing him as a hero defending Serb interests and others condemning him for his war crimes. His involvement in the Yugoslav Wars and his violent actions have left a lasting impact on the region and its people.

A possible Serbian connection is certainly an interesting theory in the Jill Dando case which can't be discounted.

Those who aren't persuaded by this theory point out though that the NATO attack came only 48 hours before Dando fronted the appeal. That seems a short space of time to agree and arrange a hit on a celebrity in a foreign country. Besides, why would Dando even be a target anyway? She was just a presenter hosting an appeal in a country on the other side of Europe. It seems a strange choice of 'revenge' victim. Another factor is that the British intelligence services allegedly never found any evidence that Dando was killed in revenge for the NATO attack.

The day after Dando's murder the police had a phone call. The transcript went like this - "Yesterday I call you to tell you to add a few numbers to your list. Because your government, and in particular your prime minister Blair, murdered, butchered 17 innocent young people. He butchered, we butcher back. The first one you had yesterday, the next one will be Tony Hall [chief executive for BBC news, and thus the man ultimately responsible for coverage of the Kosovo conflict]." The Daily Mirror also received an anonymous call claiming that two men were involved in the killing and had used a car at Bishop's Avenue, near Gowan Avenue. The Israeli intelligence services had also warned NATO that a Serbian 'hit squad' had been sent to kill someone in revenge for that NATO bombing.

Some felt that Dando's murder was uncannily similar to that of Slavko Ćuruvija. Slavko Ćuruvija was a Serbian journalist and publisher who was known for his critical reporting on former Serbian president Slobodan Milošević. He was born on September 8, 1954, in Belgrade. Ćuruvija co-founded the newspaper Dnevni Telegraf in 1994, which quickly gained popularity for its investigative journalism.

Throughout his career, Ćuruvija faced numerous threats and harassment for his outspoken criticism of the Milošević regime. He was often targeted by the state-controlled media, branded as a traitor and a Western agent. Despite this, he continued to report on corruption, war crimes, and human rights abuses. On April 11, 1999, during the NATO bombing of Serbia, Slavko Ćuruvija was assassinated outside his apartment building in Belgrade. It is believed that his murder was politically motivated, and he became one of the highest-profile journalists to be killed in post-war Serbia. Ćuruvija's death remains an unresolved case, and many believe that the perpetrators have not been brought to justice.

Despite the apparent Serbian connection, the Met Police, for reasons best known to themselves, never actually sent anyone to Serbia to investigate and still stubbornly refuse to accept this theory might be true. At the Barry George trial, his barrister Michael Mansfield claimed that Arkan had ordered a 'hit' on the BBC director general Sir John Birt as revenge but this was changed to Jill Dando because Birt's security made a hit on him too risky. "The television station was owned and run by the Milosevic family and was deliberately targeted by Nato, using a cruise missile, because it was seen as the main purveyor of Serbian state propaganda. Jill Dando by this stage had become one of the, if not the, face[s] of the BBC. In short, she was the personification and embodiment of the BBC."

Those unconvinced by the Serbian theory might ask why they went to all the trouble, expense, and risk of murdering a BBC journalist in London when there were plenty of BBC journalists in Belgrade who would have been much easier to kill. Someone like John Simpson, who has great status in the BBC, was covering the NATO bombing in Belgrade at the time. Why not kill him? John Simpson said when he spoke to Arkan about Jill Dando's murder the warlord seemed genuinely baffled by the conversation. He seemed to have no idea who Jill Dando was. He could have been faking this I suppose.

Another thing which is problematic is that Jill Dando's televised appeal was not exactly political. It was just about helping victims of a war. Dando never mentions Serbia in the appeal. So why would anyone take offence this appeal? Dando was just a presenter doing her job. She expressed no view on the war or assigned any blame to anyone. The words she spoke were written by someone else. This was a classic example of that old phrase 'don't shoot the messenger'.

If a Serb hitman only had 48 hours to shoot Jill Dando how he manage to work out where Dando's second home was so quickly and how did he know she would be there on the day in question? However, it could be that the 'hit' on Jill Dando was formulated for the refugee appeal rather than the NATO bombing and then the two become bound up to create a larger motive. An interesting alternative theory is that the murder had nothing to do with Arkan but was planned and carried out by British Serbs in London as revenge for the NATO bombing. Fulham had quite a big Serb community so this wasn't impossible. This would explain the homemade nature of the gun and knowledge the killer seemed to have of the local area in Fulham. The police never found evidence at all for this theory though. It was not something which anyone investigated extensively or heard about.

The theory that a member of the Serb community in Fulham arranged the murder is certainly interesting because it ticks a number of mystery boxes which were hitherto unticked. This would explain why the killer knew where Dando's old house in Fulham was. It seems plausible that someone in the west London/Fulham Serb community knew that Dando went back to her old house from time to time to pick up mail. It would explain why the killer seemed to have some local knowledge. While there is no evidence for this theory it is not one which can dismissed out of hand. By way of interest, the Serbian community in London is estimated to number 40,000. Serbian gangs operating in west London have been involved in drug-running and money-laundering so there would have been a dodgy criminal fraternity among them.

There is another theory concerning Jill Dando's death - although it is certainly 'out there' as far as theories go. The theory goes something like this. What if the person who killed Jill Dando had not set out to specifically kill Jill Dando? What is this was a random killer who decided to kill someone that morning and was loitering around Gowan Avenue? Jill Dando was unlucky enough to be the wrong place place at the right time. While this might sound like a preposterous theory on the face of it there are precedents for this in true crime. Take the Zodiac Killer for example.

Zodiac was the name given to a killer who operated in California in the 60s and 70s. The Zodiac Killer targeted couples who were parked up in cars. He would shoot both the man and woman. This suggested that he was an outcast in society and was embittered and angered by seeing couples in love. Another 'random' killer was David Berkowitz. Berkowitz became known as Son of Sam. He was a killer who launched random attacks in New York in 1976 and 1977. There were six confirmed victims. Berkowitz claimed that the dog (named Sam) of a neighbour was possessed by a spirit that had ordered him to kill. What if some random nutcase decided to kill Jill Dando that morning? Well, it's possible I suppose but rather unlikely all the same. How did he know she'd be at that house? How did such a person avoid ending up on the lengthy police suspect list? There are simply too many unanswered questions which abound from this theory.

CHAPTER EIGHT

There have been many unsolved murders of celebrities before - although these have tended to happen in the United States rather than Britain. Jenny Maxwell was born in New York in 1941. Blonde and cute, Maxwell was a hip and in demand actress in the late 50s and 1960s. Maxwell was friends with the doomed Sharon Tate and said to like the party life. She appeared in big television shows like The Twilight Zone and Bonanza and with Elvis in Blue Hawaii. Maxwell was also in the 1963 film Take Her, She's Mine with Jimmy Stewart.

By the mid 1960s, Maxwell's star seemed to be on the wane. She had got divorced and lost custody of her son. She was broke and her career choices had become somewhat eccentric (she appeared in a strange film called Shotgun Wedding which was written by no lesser figure than Ed Wood). Her last acting credit was a 1968 appearance in the television show The Wild Wild West. Jenny evidently just seemed to lose interest in acting. Maybe the phone just stopped ringing and she couldn't be bothered with it anymore.

In 1970, Jenny Maxwell married Ervin M. Roeder. Roeder was a lawyer and twenty years older than Jenny. It has been suggested that Jenny married Roeder because she wanted some security and stability in her life now that her acting career was history. Ervin was pretty rich so she wouldn't have to worry about money so long as he was her husband. Roeder had connections in Hollywood and was said to be something of a blowhard who liked to give the impression he had mob connections.

The marriage between Maxwell and Roeder became very tense in the end. They both had affairs and Roeder was said to have become increasingly bitter at the thought of Jenny Jenny Maxwell inheriting all of his money should he shuffle off this mortal coil before her (which seemed more than likely given that she was much younger than him). Maxwell is alleged to have wanted to leave Roeder but clung onto the marriage because her lawyer told her that she would get a bigger divorce settlement if she was married past ten years.

On June the 10th, 1981, the couple were together in Beverly Hills because Roeder had offered Jenny a lift home after she visited a hospital for minor treatment. By now they were not living together but still on fairly civil terms. In the lobby of Maxwell's Beverly Hills condo that afternoon they were both shot and killed. Jenny was shot in the head while Roeder was shot in the abdomen. It was a puzzling double murder which was never officially solved. Jenny Maxwell was 39 years-old when her life came to this gruesome and sudden end. It was a mystery to the police why anyone would want to kill a former actress and her lawyer husband.

Years later a theory on the murder surfaced. The theory alleges that Roeder hired a hitman to kill Jenny that afternoon so he wouldn't have to pay spousal support. The hitman was, according to his theory, told to make it look real and so fire a shot at Roeder too or maybe give him a non lethal injury. The hitman, if this theory is true, was obviously not a very good shot! The hitman ended up killing the person who had hired him to kill his wife!

Christa Helm was born Sandra Lynn Wohlfeil on November the 11th, 1949 in Milwaukee, Wisconsin. Helm was a bit part actress. Her roles included a small part in the TV show Wonder Woman. She was also in the 1974 horror film Legacy of Satan. Christina apparently had quite a tough childhood and suffered some abuse from the men who lived with her mother. She got pregnant when she was sixteen but the father (who was ten years older) didn't bother to stick around and accept any responsibility. Helm worked as a waitress in various places to make ends meet and nearly became a Playboy bunny at one point. A chance meeting with the singer and actor James Darren made her decide she wanted to be an actress. This ambition was modestly facilitated when she met costume designer Linny Barron.

Barron helped introduce Christa to some 'movers and shakers' and through a producer she started getting a few acting bit parts. Christa was the star of the 1974 low-budget action film Let's Go for Broke. This film didn't do much business though. Christa was dismayed when it didn't get a wide theatrical release. She inevitably moved to Los Angeles in the end and started living with a fiancer named Bernard Cornfeld in a plush mansion. Christa was, to put it mily, known as a party girl. She would sleep with anyone - especially if she thought it might help her career. It is said that when she a waitress other waitresses used to warn her about taking home men she knew nothing about but Christa never paid much attention. Christa became notorious in Hollywood for her sexual exploits. Her conquests included many famous people - including Warren Beatty, Jack Nicholson, and Mick Jagger.

Christa apparently kept a diary which detailed all of her

sexual encounters with the rich and famous. She considered this diary to be like a sort of pension or life insurance. It would make a juicy memoir or lucrative newspaper article one day. Christa is also alleged to have filmed some of her sexual encounters with the rich and famous just to make sure she had proof. There was later speculation had Christa plans to blackmail Hollywood bigwigs with her diaries and movies. Her friends are said to have warned her about speaking openly about this diary. They thought she was playing a dangerous game and would best advised to keep her mouth shut.

Despite all the Hollywood bed-hopping, Christa's career was still in no danger of taking off. She still hardly had any acting credits to her name. Her bit parts included a part as (appropriately enough) a waitress in Starsky & Hutch. Realising that her acting career had stalled and was going nowhere fast, Christa made plans to record a disco album but nothing much came of this either. It is said that she kept trying to sleep with her female backing singers. She was very ambitious and desperate to be famous but couldn't seem to find an outlet or opening for a career in Hollywood.

In 1976, Christa is said to have dated the permanently tanned and always dapper actor George Hamilton. She was also said to be involved with the disc jockey Frankie Crocker. Christa was also linked to actors and producers. She evidently still had hopes that her acting career might yet get a boost from one of these connections. For a time, Christa lived in a loft with a woman named Patty Collins. They were also lovers but those who knew Christa later said they felt that Patty was trouble. They detected a tension between the two women and said that Christa planned to end the friendship.

On the night of February the 12th, 1977, Christa went to a Hollywood party in Laurel Canyon with her roommate Stephanie. At some point, Christa left the party. She was later found stabbed to death outside of her agent Sandy Smith's house. She was 27 years-old (there's that old curse again - a LOT of famous people, if one could call Christa famous, have died at the age of 27). Christa was stabbed 23 times and also beaten with a heavy object. Sandy Smith was allegedly asleep and heard nothing. Christa's blood splattered body was found by a young man who walked through that street shortly after the murder.

The tyre marks and abrupt fashion in which Christa's car was parked that night led police to suspect that someone was following her and she was trying to get to Smith's house for safety. Residents of the street told police they heard what sounded like an argument coming from outside and then a scream. The knife which carried out the murder was never found. In fact, the case was never solved at all.

There wasn't much media coverage of Christa's murder at all. She wasn't famous enough to warrant much ink. As for suspects, well, they certainly exist. The agent Sandy Smith was later found to be telling an untruth when he said he was asleep as Christa was being stabbed outside his house. He actually had guests that night. What was he trying to hide by this lie? Those who knew Christa thought the prime suspect was her old flame Patsy Collins - who was a backup singer and lover to Christa.

The story goes that Patsy was furious when Christa went cool on her and said she wasn't even gay anyway. Patsy, according to this theory, stabbed Christa to death in revenge. Another suspect is Rudy Mozella - who was a keyboard player in Christa's disco band. She was hoarding some cocaine for him. The theory in this instance is that Christa used some of the cocaine herself and he murdered her as a consequence. Believe it or not, one of the people interviewed by the police in relation to this murder was Tony Sirico - who later became famous playing Paulie Walnuts in The Sopranos. Sirico was one of the last people to visit Christa before her death.

Christa's diary and tapes detailing her sexual encounters went missing after her death. This has obviously led to speculation that she was killed by some Hollywood figure who feared that she might release embarrassing scandalous information about him. The main suspect though is still generally judged to have been Patsy Collins. One of the main reasons for this is not just their storied history together but also because Patsy suspiciously vanished after the murder.

The police never spoke to Patsy Collins about this murder because they had had no idea where she was. Modern forensic testing on this case has suggested that Christa had female DNA under her nails when she died. This would obviously tally with the Patsy Collins theory. Christa's daughter Nicole continues to work towards some sort of belated resolution in this case. She hasn't given up trying to solve the riddle of her mother's awful murder.

Ronni Sue Chasen was born in New York in 1946. She was the sister of the cult horror director and writer Larry Cohen. Chasen was an aspiring actress as a young women but eventually moved behind the scenes and became a Hollywood publicist. Her clients included the likes of Michael Douglas, John Williams, and Natalie Wood. Chasen's specific skill was in orchestrating Oscar campaigns for movies or clients. She was exceptional in these duties and a tireless and cheerful presence in the Los Angeles studio film community.

There are many photographs online of famous faces clutching Oscars with Chasen by their side. It was her hard work behind the scenes promoting movies and stars that made many of these triumphs possible. Chasen was brilliant at her job and loved it too. She loved working in the film industry and never wanted to retire.

On November the 16th, 2010, the 64 year-old Chasen attended the gltzy premiere of the Christina Aguilera and Cher film Burlesque. After midnight, Chasen headed home - which entailed a drive through a wealthy enclave of Beverly Hills. Near the intersection of Whittier Drive and Sunset Boulevard at around 12-30 am, four gunshots were fired through the front passenger seat window of Chasen's Mercedes-Benz car. It is believed the shots were most likely fired as Chasen slowed down in preparation to make a turn.

Two of the bullets struck Chasen in the chest and one hit her in the arm. None of these three bullets were fatal in and of themselves but sadly the same could not be said of a fourth bullet. This bullet struck Chasen in the heart. The bullet to the heart was the killer blow. After the shots, Chasen's car carried on moving for about a third of a mile before it struck a pole and the airbag was deployed. Chasen was obviously in no condition to either steer or stop. She only had minutes to live.

Police officers were quickly on the scene because the sound of gunshots had been reported to them by local residents. Chasen was taken to Cedars-Sinai Medical Center and pronounced dead at 1-12 am. Those who knew Chasen were shocked and upset. She was always such a nice person so it seemed both bizarre and unfair that she had been shot to death. There were two obvious question now. Who had killed Ronni Sue Chasen and why? The early theories concerning Chasen's murder were that this was potentially a violent attempted carjacking or maybe just a random shooting involving some troubled David Berkowitz style lunatic.

Some suggested Chaen's death might have been a consequence of some sort of road rage incident but there was never any evidence to support this. The problem with these theories was that incidents like this were very rare in that specific area. At the time of her murder, Chasen was driving through an area where all the houses were worth many millions. This wasn't a violent crime infested area where people got shot on a daily basis. This was an area with much security and a Batphone type hotline to the police.

The police suspect was a local man named Harold Martin Smith. Smith had some criminal convictions on his slate. He lived in a cheap apartment block in Los Angeles. When the police went to speak to Smith though he pulled out a gun and shot himself. The authorities seemed to conclude that this suicide proved he was guilty of the murder. The police would later say that the gun used in the suicide was the same sort of gun that killed Ronnie Chasen.

Many armchair detectives who have studied this case though contend that Smith probably had nothing to do with Chasen's murder. There was no surveillance or forensic evidence linking him to the crime. The swanky area where Chasen was shot was full of security cameras and yet the police did not pick up any footage of a lone black man (Smith was black) suspiciously driving or lurking around. Others pointed out the rather sad but obvious fact that a black man in this well heeled street at some unearthly hour probably would have attracted the attention of the police.

The police, in what felt like a contradiction to their earlier stance, later seemed to come to similar conclusions and suggest that Chasen's death was just a tragic random incident that will probably never be solved. Some of the frustrated friends and colleagues of Chasen felt that the murder investigation was rather lackadaisical and that the police were too quick to wash their hands of this case.

Because of Chasen's line of work, a number of conspiracy theories concerning her death have inevitably abounded. These include the theory that she was killed by a Russian hitman after a film funded by Russian investment money didn't see a profit. Another theory is that Chasen was killed by a rival movie publicist company because she was too good at her job! There is another theory too that Chasen was murdered after an art deal went wrong. The notion that Chasen was murdered by art dealers sounds as far-fetched as any of the movies she promoted during her career.

Because Chasen was killed with hollow point bullets (which are even more lethal than ordinary bullets) this has only fanned the flames of conspiracies. Some of these claim she was killed by a professional hitman (as opposed to a lone criminal or lunatic). It should be stressed though that the police regarded all of these conspiracy theories to be nonsense. The sadly departed Ronnie Chasen was laid to rest at Hillside Memorial Park and Mortuary in Los Angeles. Among those who attended her funeral were Elliott Gould, Amy Pascal, Joe Roth, Leonard Maltin, Kathleen Kennedy, Robert Forster, and Buzz Aldrin.

The investigation into the murder of Jill Dando remains open and the actual truth has yet to be proven. Hamish Campbell, the police officer who was in charge of investigating the Jill Dando murder, still stubbornly insists that Barry George was the killer. It is doubtful that many would agree with him on this. Nick Ross also continues to believe that Barry George or a Barry George type character was the killer. Ross has often stated that he believes the theories about hitmen, Serbs, the Russian Mafia etc are simply silly conspiracy theories. Ross actually likens the murder of Jill Dando to the murder of John Lennon. He believes Jill was probably killed by some nutty fan of hers. Ross believes Barry George - or someone like Barry George - was Mark Chapman.

There is another conspiracy theory we haven't mentioned yet which relates to Daniel Morgan. The murder of Daniel Morgan is one of the most notorious unsolved murders in British history. Daniel Morgan was a private investigator who was found dead with an axe embedded in his head in a pub car park in London in 1987. At the time of his murder, Morgan was investigating corruption within London's Metropolitan Police. He had uncovered evidence of police involvement in drug trafficking and other criminal activities, and it is believed that this may have been a motive for his killing. It is suspected that his work as a private investigator may have also put him in contact with dangerous individuals who wanted to silence him.

The murder investigation faced significant obstacles from the start. The initial police inquiry was plagued with corruption and incompetence, with evidence and witnesses ignored or lost. There have been many allegations of police corruption and involvement in covering up the murder. This has led to multiple failed investigations and inquiries into the case over the years. Despite five police investigations and several prosecutions, no one has ever been successfully convicted for Morgan's murder. The case has been marred by corruption, obstruction, and allegations of collusion between criminals and law enforcement. The lack of accountability and justice for the murder of Daniel Morgan has become a symbol of institutional failure within the British criminal justice system.

Efforts to bring justice to the Morgan family have continued for decades. In 2011, a panel was set up to examine the case, and it concluded that the Metropolitan Police were guilty of "institutional corruption." In 2021, an independent panel released a damning report that concluded there was "significant" and "extensive" police corruption involved in the investigation. The murder of Daniel Morgan remains unsolved, and his family continues to fight for justice and truth. The case represents not only a tragic loss of life but also highlights the challenges and failures of the criminal justice system in addressing police corruption.

There is a theory that Jill Dando had also uncovered corruption in the Met Police and media and was therefore 'silenced' to prevent her from doing anything about this. It would be fair to say that this theory is speculative and not exactly watertight. Jill Dando was not an investigative reporter. At the time of her death she was hosting The Antiques Inspectors and being lined up for the BAFTAS. She wasn't Bob Woodward. The idea that behind the scenes she was a private eye exposing all these conspiracies and drawing the fury of the establishment is rather hard to believe. If you go down this rabbit hole you end up back in the crazy and grim world of conspiracy theories where everything (and by everything they usually mean everything left-wing or Jewish) is a paedophile conspiracy or an economic conspiracy. You might as will ask Alex Jones or David Icke to investigate Jill Dando's murder for all the sense you'll get.

So, we now end up back where we started. Who killed Jill

Dando? Although some still think there is something fishy about Barry George and believe he could well have been the killer it is difficult to concur with this assessment. George certainly ticked a number of boxes - chiefly the fact that he lived in Fulham close to Dando. However, one of the most salient problems with the theory that it was Barry George all along is that the home loaded ammunition and nature of the gun used in the murder would have required a certain standard of craftsmanship and expertise. There is no evidence at all that Barry George possessed this craftsmanship and expertise. This is a man who could barely wash some dishes or change a lightbulb. The notion that he was some sort of MacGyver style weapons expert is fanciful to say the least. The eyewitness statements did not match Barry George either and we've already spoken in depth about how weak the firearms residue evidence was.

Barry George was clearly a troubled man who was a nuisance to a great many women. You might say that the several years he served in prison for Jill Dando's murder was some sort of cosmic karma for all the bad things he had done. His release though was justified because there was insufficient evidence to say with any certainty at all that he had killed Jill Dando. It seems logical then to remove Barry George from the list of possibilities. The 'lone nutcase' (for want of a better phrase) theory favoured by the police and Nick Ross can't be completely discounted but it does seem highly debatable. Why wasn't this person captured? Murderous stalkers like this would surely draw attention to themselves sooner or later. And wouldn't such a person have killed again?

The killer of Jill Dando pushed her head right down until it was almost on the ground and then shot into her left temple. All of this ensured a swift death out of sight and negated the noise the gun would make. The charge of the gun (which makes the noise) was muffled by happening so close to the victim. These details do not suggest that an amateur committed this murder. The killer also escaped with surprising ease - leaving only a trickle of confused and inconsistent eyewitness sightings in his wake. It is believed that the killer probably turned left after the murder. It seems highly probable that the killer had an accomplice waiting in a car. If the killer sat in this car before the murder that would explain why they were not seen loitering outside. Though this was a west London street it was surprisingly empty that morning. There were no shops on the street and many residents were at work.

If the killer had an accomplice in a car this would explain how they escaped the scene. The killer might then have left the car and disappeared via public transport while the accomplice perhaps went his own seperate way and disposed of the weapon. This theory solves one of the biggest mysteries in the case. That is how did the killer know Jill Dando would be at her old home in Fulham and why didn't he kill her in Chiswick? The accomplice theory proposes there were two men in contact through radio. One is staking out Dando's Chiswick home and one is keeping an eye on her old home in Fulham. They deduce that she has gone shopping in Hammersmith and is on her way to Fulham. Therefore they both meet up in Fulham and stake out Gowan Avenue. They have sprung a deadly trap.

If this is what happened then who were the 'hitmen'? A hit squad from Serbia? Serbs from London? While this is possible it seems more likely that it was British criminals who did the hit. It is true that it is atypical and unusual from criminals to target a public figure but Crimewatch was basically a show which asked the public to 'snitch' (to use criminal jargon) on criminals. Criminals were put behind bars due to investigations on Crimewatch. Is it really that far-fetched to think that someone in the criminal community was so annoyed by the ramifications of something on Crimewatch that they decided to take revenge on one of the presenters on the show?

If this scenario is what really happened then why not murder Nick Ross rather than Jill Dando? Well, who knows? Maybe they though Jill Dando was an easier target. Maybe they thought Dando (who was more famous than Nick Ross because she did loads of other stuff besides Crimewatch) would be making more of a statement. With respect to Nick Ross, he had a much lower profile than Jill Dando. If we dismiss the silly conspiracy theories we are left with two options. Jill Dando was either killed by a disturbed stalker or it was some sort of criminal hit. The stalker theory is possible but there was something quick and clean about the murder which makes one question this theory.

Would a crazed Jill Dando stalker have been savvy enough to push her head to the floor and shoot her in the temple so that the explosive gases of the gun were muffled? There was certainly no sexual motive in the murder. It was just a quick shot to the head - even though the 'Jill Dando obsessed stalker' had a window of opportunity to push Dando into the house. Despite the reactivated weapon the murder seemed to fit the MO of someone who knew what they were doing. Someone who had done this type of thing before. Could a character like Barry George really have done this murder? The poor man could barely walk in a straight line let alone sprint from a crime scene.

If we then continue down this path of feeling the murder seemed more 'professional' than 'amateur' we then have to make a choice between British criminals and Serb revenge. The latter is a possibility and believed by many but it would certainly have been easier for British criminals to kill Dando because they would have been able to do more research on her movements and routines. They would have been able to hire people who knew west London like the back of their hand. One of the salient reasons why the 'professional' theory is compelling is that British criminals and Serbs can be be ascribed a motive. The respective motives are Crimewatch and the television appeal/NATO. It's a lot more difficult to do that with the 'lone nutter' theory. As we have seen, despite a lengthy investigation, a conviction, and two trials the police never actually came up with a motive for why Barry George would want to shoot Jill Dando.

We know why Mark Chapman (as disturbed and delusional as he was) shot John Lennon. Chapman, obsessed by The Catcher in the Rye, thought that Lennon (of whom Chapman was a big fan) was a phoney. We know why John Hinckley Jr tried to kill Ronald Reagan. Hinckley developed an unhealthy obsession with the teenage actress Jodie Foster after she played an underage prostitute in the famous Martin Scorsese film Taxi Driver. Hinckley made repeated (and predictably unsuccessful) attempts to contact Foster and became so frustrated by his inability to make her take any notice of him that he decided to assassinate Ronald Reagan in mimicry of the alienated vigilante Travis Bickle in Taxi Driver. Hinckley, completely detached from reality, thought this murder would impress Foster and that the actress would finally notice him. But why would Barry George kill Jill Dando? His flat dredged up no evidence at all that he'd ever given her much thought.

Investigative journalist Mark Williams-Thomas spoke to a figure in the criminal underworld who was on the police list of suspects back in 1999. This former criminal said that the murder of Jill Dando struck him as a professional operation and that he had a good idea who was behind it. "There are some very nasty horrible people out there," said Williams-Thomas, "criminals – and the crucial element, from their point of view, is that they may perceive that Crimewatch puts criminals away, therefore putting their friends and colleagues away, and I think that was the reason." My own view, as we draw to a conclusion, is that this theory is the most likely and most logical. It was a 'hit' by the criminal fraternity in Britain for something related to Crimewatch. Case closed? Well, not really. It's just a theory but certainly the most compelling one in the competing swirl of explanations for why a Songs of Praise presenter was gunned down on her doorstep one morning many years ago. One day we may get the truth and the file on this bizarre murder can finally be closed.